To one "sinner" ⌁ W9-BIM-335 ⌁
who loves you very much.
Christmas, 1964

Tommy Harrell

*For Preachers and Other Sinners*

GERALD KENNEDY

# For
# Preachers
## and Other Sinners

*Harper & Row, Publishers*

NEW YORK, EVANSTON, AND LONDON

LIBRARY OF CONGRESS CATALOG CARD NUMBER: 64-14379

I-O

*This is for my friend and colleague*

DONALD HARVEY TIPPETT

# Contents

# Preface

In 1960 I was invited to contribute a regular feature to the Christian Century *Pulpit*—a monthy magazine for preachers. Under the improbable name of G. Hobab Kish, I have written "The Mourners Bench" without any feeling of making a major contribution to either the Church or the ministry. But writing it has given me personal pleasure, and at certain times of frustration it has been better than an hour on the couch.

Letters began to arrive at my office commenting on the sentiments of Kish, which I merely acknowledged and promised to see that he was informed. My friends would remark that Kish was right on the beam last month or that old Hobab was lost in the woods. I professed little interest in him, but nobody was fooled. A man's style, prejudices, pet causes, all betray him. And so "The Mourners Bench" has pleased some and infuriated others. It has probably bored some also, but they never wrote.

The purpose has been to stimulate. None of these pieces is objective, and none of them is a serious, scholarly presentation of a subject. They often go against the prevailing opinion. They spring out of personal experience and personal observation of a good many ministries during the past decade or so. I am afraid that some of them have been inspired by annoyances, irritations, and impatience. At any rate, some of what is included here has appeared already in print, and I express my thanks to Dr. Kyle Haselden, editor of *The Pulpit,* for permission to include the material in this book.

I would feel bad if anyone interpreted the complaints expressed as indicating a growing pessimism. Truly my enthusiasm for the Church and the ministry is more exuberant than ever. A man critcizes only

*ix*

that which concerns him deeply, and besides, what follows is mostly a testimony to the greatness of the pastor of the local church. Preaching is still my first love; preachers are my favorite people; and the Church, in my judgment, is the last, best hope.

GERALD KENNEDY

*Hollywood, California*

*For Preachers and Other Sinners*

# 1: *Conferences*

I have just returned from a church conference and I am feeling mighty low. Brethren, let us admit that such affairs do not represent the Church at its best. I must confess there seems to be no substitute for such meetings, and it looks as if we shall have them to the end of time, which is as long as God promised to maintain the Church. But I wonder if God does not feel like making a motion to adjourn and go home—not once but many times in these ecclesiastical gatherings.

For one thing, there are the boys who are always speaking for the record. They want to be sure the journal will contain some of their flights of eloquence so the folks back home will know their delegate is a leader. These speeches hardly ever say anything and are seldom made if the issue is controversial. That is not the kind of record they are speaking for. Resolutions to honor somebody or to pray for something are pretty safe, and these subjects are nearly all pre-empted by the boys who want to say later, "Look, Ma, I was speaking."

There is another large class of orators who are running for something. You cannot be elected a bishop by keeping your mouth shut, or at least that is the theory. So along toward the end of the conference these birds arise and spread their wings. They just want to assure everybody that they love everybody and they appreciate everything. The carefully prepared extemporaneous remarks are full of general literary allusions and nearly always contain a poem or two. I could not prove this, but I would wager two to one that the reason why some candidates have been running for years and never get very close to the Promised Land is these speeches.

Then come the specialists in delay after the previous question has been voted. The chairman points out that the motion is not debatable, but they want to ask a question. My reaction is that after the long debate a fellow who still does not know what the motion means is too stupid to be a delegate. But these boys are subtle. They want to get in another little argument by way of a question, and too many chairmen, not desiring to be arbitrary, let them get way with it.

It is amazing to note how few do nearly all of the talking. Out of a thousand delegates, fifty men will monopolize 90 per cent of the time. Are these the wisest, the biggest, the greatest men? Dear friends, they are not. It is not an iron bound rule, but it is generally true that the best men speak seldom and speak briefly. Not so anxious for publicity, they do their work quietly and humbly. They are the boys in the back room planning some godly strategy to move the Church along another foot. But when they speak, people listen.

There were two members of a long church conference who went to visit a grove of California sequoias before going home. One looked in silence at the majesty of a tree over three thousand years old. "Bill," he said finally, "it just goes to show what God can do when there is no one around to move the previous question."

Some time ago I was in Istanbul enjoying the hospitality of the Eastern Orthodox Church. One of the bishops accompanied us to the Halke Theological Seminary on an island in the Sea of Marmora. Early in the morning the boat stopped at a little town across from Istanbul called Chalcedon. It was an ordinary-looking place, and I asked the bishop if this was where the great council had been held. He said it was. The date was 541. I read about it later and found its conclusions pleased hardly anyone and its debates were often bitter. You know what I think? I think that many of those six hundred bishops felt as discouraged when that council broke up as this poor old preacher feels right now. But God moves in a mysterious way, even through the conferences of His Church.

## 2: *Words*

There is a story about an author who needed money and wired his publisher, "How much advance will you give for a novel of sixty thousand words?" The publisher wired back, "How big are the words?" Some of the stuff put out today seems to emphasize bulk and nothing else. How many books are written that would be much better if they were condensed and shortened! We develop jargon for every intellectual discipline, so that two sentences will reveal what school the writer comes from and what high-sounding nonsense will be used to cover his lack of thought. Words are chosen with paralysis in their muscles and leukemia in their blood. Lifeless, dull, abstract, academic, they kill any interest a man might have in the subject. The mimeograph machine (that invention of the devil) enables every bore to spread his dullness across the earth and so mutilate and cheapen words that they rouse hatred, or worse, go unnoticed.

The mimeographed tripe that comes across my desk and slides rapidly into the wastebasket is simply terrifying. Every committee sends its minutes and every organization passes resolutions. Every secretary and bureaucrat sitting around with nothing to do suddenly gets the great idea: "Let's send out another mailing!" I can only assume that everybody is a frustrated author, and will get his dull words and tiresome style on paper if it kills him, and sometimes I wish it would. There is a law—call it Kennedy's Law—that the less an organization is needed, the more printed matter it will distribute. And the corollary is that the less there is accomplished, the fancier the annual report.

But brethren, before you lose all control, turn back to the Bible. One of my former colleagues on a theological seminary faculty has pointed out that while the Greeks are a people of the eye, the Jews are a

*3*

Tommy Harrell

people of the ear. They have a sense of words and their language is alive. They speak, they tell, they announce, they proclaim. God has told them what is good, and He has commanded them what to do. There in the Bible you will find speech that is living and vital and unforgettable and inescapable. The Old Testament tells the Joseph story in thirteen brief chapters, while Thomas Mann takes four volumes. Modern novelists write long books about biblical characters and make one-tenth the impression made by the short verses in the Bible. Here is the Book that knows about the miracle and wonder of words. "In the beginning was the Word."

Classrooms are the worst places so far as dead language is concerned. The educational experts develop a speech that is fit for no habitation save a cemetery. Any man who gets in some theoretical ivory tower is doomed to talk ultimately like a walking ghost. It is in the market place, the home, at the ball park, the shop, the church, that language is alive. Every man who would speak or write must be with all kinds of real people in all kinds of real situations. John Wesley and one of his preachers came upon two women quarreling near Billingsgate. Their language was forceful but not polite. The preacher suggested moving along, but Wesley said, "Stay, Sammy, stay, and learn to preach." Woe unto us when we withdraw to our closets and converse only with our own kind.

I listened to a long-winded speech on the floor of a conference, not long ago. Turning to a friend of mine from Texas, I asked what the speech was all about. He answered: "A friend of his has his tail caught in a crack, and he wants us to help him get it out." How pointed! How adequate! How fine!

It may be that one of this generation's greatest crimes is the debasing of our language. When I think of TV commercials, I get sick to my stomach. The Madison Avenue boys have done more to reveal the essential tawdriness of our civilization than any other single force. What shall our defense be when we stand to be judged by the One who said: "I tell you, on the day of judgment men will render account for every careless word they utter; for by your words you will be justified, and by your words you will be condemned" (Matt. 12:36-37).

4

# 3: *Alibis*

The other day we were all celebrating Scott Carpenter's successful triple orbit of the earth and his safe return. I got to thinking about the long and hard road American science had followed to this event. I remembered all the failures, all the delays, all the last-minute disappointments. Yet during that whole time I could not remember any scientist blaming the defeats on ill fortune. Did any of them announce that they were the victims of bad breaks? Did anyone say that those Russians had been just plain lucky? The whole idea seems completely incongruous in this realm, for we knew that we were in second place because we had started too late with too little.

Then my little mind began to consider church affairs—since preachers always ultimately come around to that subject. Do we react to our failures in our field as the scientists do in theirs? Don't make me laugh! Every church has a perfect alibi to explain why another is moving while it is not. Why that other bunch have the right location, and we are half a block off the boulevard. They have a new educational building and we do not even have a bowling alley. They have cushions on the pews, while the backs on ours hit you in just the wrong place. Their parking lot is adequate, while our lot is crowded. Their community is completely homogeneous, while ours has some people with lower incomes. A recent survey shows that we have 2 per cent more Catholics and .5 per cent more Jews. By this time you are worn out with the tragic story of injustice, and tears begin to run down your cheeks.

If we are suffering a decrease in church school attendance, you will listen to a string of reasons which will almost convince you that the figures are a mirage. Compare the present situation with 1904 and you will see that in some strange way we are making progress even when we lose enrollment. You will not hear a word about the Sunday school being so dull that the children are bored and attend only when threatened with a whip. Nothing is said about the possibility that the teaching has so little vitality that parents conclude it makes very little difference whether their offspring attend or not. Indeed, you will hear everything under the sun except that the church school may be a wash-out.

And when it comes to the preacher—ah, brethren, this will wring your heart! The system held him back, and while he ought to be in First Church, he was penalized by jealous officials. He spoke like a prophet, and his people stopped coming. A cantankerous layman who was present in every church he ever served undermined his leadership. Strange, but in every congregation he has had the same experiences for the last thirty years. Those other successful fellows? Compromisers—politicians—wire-pullers—lucky! Not once in all his ministry did this fellow ever admit, "Maybe I goofed. Maybe I give the impression of being arrogant, tactless, and brittle."

Anyway, I keep thinking about those scientists. It might be that a dose of their spirit would be good for us. There was one in the New Testament who tried to alibi his failure and was thrown into outer darkness. How about a moratorium on ministerial alibis and explanations that do not explain?

# 4: *Trouble*

Most instructional books seem to assume the worst. You are in trouble and they show you the way out of it. Or you made a mistake and they tell how to correct it. Apparently these books are written by pessimistic fellows. But a sports writer said the other day that he preferred Sam Snead's counsel on how to handle the rough: "Don't get in it."

When some of our courses for preachers' wives are over, I wonder that any young woman has the courage to go further on the ministerial road. She is warned of all the sand traps, all the trees in the way, and the impossible narrowness of the fairway. She must begin to assume that the whole course is nothing but trouble and that she will not have one straight drive down the middle during the whole game. A fine minister's wife I know tried to share the joy of the parsonage with a group of students' wives one time, but they thought she was lying, or at least covering up the actual situation. They had been thoroughly indoctrinated in the philosophy of the rough.

Any man can prove that the ministry is an impossible job. Read what some of the modern books are saying about the task of the preacher. How can you speak to the old and the young, the wise and the simple, the healthy and the sick? How can you break the defenses of the contemporary mind? St. Paul's reference to "the foolishness of preaching" sounds very tame compared with these diatribes. The boys are so discouraged before they start that the first adversity throws them into despair.

There are, of course, pitfalls for the minister and his family. Any job as demanding and wonderful as the ministry is bound to present all kinds of hazards. But most of them can be avoided with some common sense and the gift of God's grace. Some are not really very serious and add zest to the game. Still others will prove to be deepening experiences of the spirit, and in many cases the laymen will help the young man for they know how easy it is to miss your aim.

If our ideas of our work are small, every experience in the rough will be a major crisis. This is certainly one place in life where the principle of relativity holds true. The importance of our calling will determine largely how we react to disappointments and failure. The storm will break the brittle trunk but only bend the resilient one.

So it seems to me that more time spent in enlarging our vision of the ministry is better than so much effort expended in writing directions of how to cope with its problems. The man who feels honored by his calling will not have nearly as much trouble in it as the one who approaches it suspiciously. The fellow who expects to enjoy the game probably will.

I wonder if we ought not to be preaching a message of joy more than we do. I hear sermons which are like the instructional books—all warnings about mishaps. But Christians have always impressed their neighbors as having experienced as absurd kind of joy which the world cannot give or take away, or understand. They know about a divine protection that covers them day and night. They testify to the feeling of being held up by everlasting arms. If the preacher can first experience this in his own life and escape the contemporary temptation of self-pity, he may proclaim a message of power which keeps people out of the rough. Let us stand and sing:

> *This is my Father's world:*
> *Why should my heart be sad?*
> *The Lord is King: let the heavens ring!*
> *God reigns: let the earth be glad!*

# 5: *Unchanging*

I see by the papers that a long-cherished chemical theory has been overthrown. It seems that the so-called "inert" gases will combine with other chemical elements after all, and now a whole host of new chemical compounds are made possible. Thousands of scientists have assumed this was impossible, and now the textbooks have to be revised, and what Johnny learned last year was true he must learn this year is false. Ah, this wonderful scientific age that has the answers to everything!

The Bible, however, runs through the same old editions year after year, century after century. Our language changes, and now and then we find a little more light to shed on the text, but revisions never change anything basic. The headline hunters try to stir up the possibility of finding something new that will affect the Book radically; but nothing ever comes of it. They tried to suggest that the discovery of the Dead Sea Scrolls might force a reappraisal of the Gospels, but while we are getting more information about religion and life at the time of Jesus, the New Testament light shines on unabated.

A few books have been written on what the space age might do to the tenets of orthodox Christianity—as if the new concepts of the immensity of space might embarrass our ideas of God. Or somebody now and then wonders what Christians will do if there should prove to be creatures as smart or smarter than we are on other planets. While we had to adjust ourselves once before to the idea that the earth is not the center of the universe, and we are now learning that the universe is bigger than we thought, most of us have never doubted that God is big enough for whatever we may find.

Just about every doubt that can be raised has become commonplace to Christians. Every attack on the Scriptures that could be launched has been tried, not once, but many times. If the Christian faith has any cracks in it, they would have been discovered after two thousand years of searching. If the biblical affimations could not stand the nosing around of all kinds of smart alecks, they would have crumbled long ago. So it is nice to go to bed at night without any fear that the next morning's headline may read: LONG-CHERISHED BIBLICAL THEORY PROVED FALSE.

This has a meaning for preachers which is not always recognized or appreciated. For one thing, let us root our sermons in the eternal truths of the Bible. The disillusionment that comes to the poor fellow who looks back over his old sermons is due to the transitoriness of so much of the material. The idea sounded good at the time, but it was really not very deep, and you wonder how you could have labored it for a half hour before a congregation of helpless people. That striking reference to the headline of the week would have been better forgotten, for it was not the important news of the time. In fact, the whole thing was of such passing significance that you hope you do not sink that low again.

It means a great deal to be dealing with the timeless. The outward circumstances change, but the heart of man, the needs of society, the grace of God, the Incarnation, are the same yesterday, today, and forever. I wonder if we ever pause to consider the dignity of our calling, which proclaims the Word beyond change and death. Stand on your feet, men, and stop acting like commentators. Be prophets!

Every time a long-accepted theory explodes, I have an inner, secret, faintly malicious joy. We are not as smart as we think we are, and all our pride is for fools. But he who serves the God of Abraham and preaches the Gospel of His Son will never be confounded. Amen!

# 6: *Awards*

Awards are among the least expensive and yet most acceptable gifts in the world. Offer a preacher either a large honorarium or another honorary degree, and nine times out of ten he will take the degree. Some little one-horse organization with enough money to have a parchment printed or a plaque engraved will have no trouble getting first-rate speakers for their annual meetings if they will give an award. It does not matter much what it is for. Maybe a fellow helped a lady across the street, or slowed up for cross traffic, or said a good word for freedom. Give him an award and then sit back and collect a thousand dollars' worth of service from him. Brethren, it's a racket, but it's wonderful!

It means we like a little recognition. Even in materialistic America, money is not enough. We would rather have a medal or a citation. Some of the Hollywood moguls would not be caught dead in a meeting of the Society for the Advancement of Literacy in Lower Slobovia. But let the Society offer the poor millionaire producer a two-dollar piece of paper saying that he produced the best picture of the year, and he will be there on time and even pay for his dinner. Which is to say that money is dandy, but to have one's work recognized is much better.

Now all of this is overlooked too much in the church. Laymen can fall into the habit of ferreting out a minister's weak point and blowing it up all out of proportion. All they can see finally is this admittedly weak quality, and if they try hard enough, they can give the congregation this same astigmatism. Sure he has weak points. So has every man, and so will every minister who ever serves that church. In my moments of honesty (too rare), I marvel at how people have put up with me. But we must shore up our preachers on the weak side and admire their strong side.

It is good business to give a preacher a raise and tell him that his accomplishments are appreciated. A little dinner and a little bragging will get more results than all the criticism in the world. Nothing makes a man work harder than to have somebody say he is doing a good job. He goes farther faster with a little sweetening in his diet, while a constant sourness is like brakes on his machine.

Preachers need to learn this lesson, too. We can become a thankless lot, complaining about the laymen who are not of much account and overlooking the laymen who make the church great. Plan some recognition for the boys who do the visiting and the chairmen who raise the budgets. Write a note of thanks to the president of the woman's society, or better yet, send her some flowers. Most of our people never get any notice, and to have their names in the paper is a rare experience. Let the church hand out a few awards to the plain saints who will never make *Who's Who* but whose names are written in the Lamb's Book of Life.

Awards are wonderful to get and they are wonderful to give. Then when you have to speak like a prophet, the people will remember the shepherd. Strange that so many of us in the ministry preach this on Sunday but never take the time to practice it on Monday.

# 7: *Cafeterias*

The other day a friend of mine took his small son to lunch at a cafeteria. He was not paying much attention and found the little rascal had passed everything but the desserts, of which he had taken five. Once on the tray, there was no way to get them back on the counter without a terrific row. My friend tries to be a modern parent, and he was quite upset at what this experience does to the theory that children ought to make their own decisions.

I began to think about this in education. My schooling began about the time the curriculm was supposed to be a kind of cafeteria line where the students made their own selections. I took Spanish instead of Latin because somebody told me it was easier. It has handicapped me all my life to have no basic knowledge of Latin constructions.

We are still in the clutches of "nondirective" counseling and relationships. It is supposed to be a crime to make a suggestion or try to influence anybody. The preacher as a counselor must not let his convictions show. But Chesterton said he did not want to be influenced; he wanted to be commanded. I feel the same way. Whenever a fellow starts to be "nondirective" with me, I get away from him just as fast as I can.

Of course this spirit of the age has entered religion. There are church programs that offer everything from dancing lessons to flower arrangement. The theory seems to be that the church exists to furnish everything that people think they might like to try. There is plenty of activity, all right, but when these Christians get into real trouble they are no better equipped to deal with it than a faithful Rotarian. The cafeteria-church panders to the unbalanced desires of man's immaturity.

Look at the pulpit! Here are men giving the people what they want. They trim their sails to fit the wind, and their pious mouthings give about as much strengthening to the spiritual muscles as cream puffs. The babes of the Gospel prefer milk, so give them milk! The solid food which Paul speaks of to the Corinthians will never be digested by our spiritual weaklings. For we are content to let them remain babes. There are church members who have been eating pious dessert for years, and the only reason they are not dead from indigestion is that they go to church about once a month.

Thomas Merton in *The Seven Storey Mountain* says he was a student in spiritual turmoil and went to a Protestant church in New York. He writes: "The minister of the church was very friendly and used to get into conversations about intellectual matters and modern literature . . . It seemed he counted very much on that sort of thing—considered it an essential part of his ministry. That was precisely one of the things that made the experience of going to his church such a sterile one for me. It was politics that he talked about; not religion and God. You felt that the man did not know his vocation, did not know what he was supposed to be."

Dear brethren, scare them and shock them next Sunday morning with a "Thus saith the Lord: . . ." Tell them that Christ came not to give them what they want, but what they need. No more cafeteria lines, but the King's banquet! No more unbalanced, sickly, secularized meals! Lord, send us some spiritual dietitians with both grace and courage.

# 8 · *Tongues*

A fellow came to see me the other day and told me about his experience of speaking in tongues. Seems that at last he has found the answer to his problems, and at last the power of the Holy Spirit has entered into him. He told me about a magazine being published by the glossolalia brethren and how the movement is spreading in such unlikely places as the Episcopalian and Lutheran churches. I was quite impressed and began a little investigation on my own.

I found a few churches split right down the middle over this subject. I could not find any clear evidence of ineffective ministers made effective. The fruits of the experience evidently are personal, for no one could give me any particular social results which an outsider might observe. But all of this may be too recent and sporadic to produce the signs I sought. I decided to look to the past.

Paul had the experience of "speaking in tongues," but he took a dim view of public demonstrations, especially when no one could interpret what was being said. He put the gift at the bottom of his list and apparently never regarded it as either essential or very significant. The experience at Pentecost was an actual talking in other languages which men from other lands could understand.

Great revivals have been accompanied by these manifestations, but a man like John Wesley discouraged such outbursts because they threatened to get out of control. For the life of me, I cannot see that any of the lasting effects of the revivals were associated with or dependent on "talking in tongues." Indeed, I cannot see that the last two thousand years of Christian history show anything constructive resulting from this movement.

But there is a gift of tongues which I covet for myself and for my brethren. I wish the Holy Spirit might grant the gift of speaking in clear English. Some congregations might not recognize that their pastor had had any new gift of "tongues," since they have never understood him anyway. Oh, that we might labor for simple words, organized thought, and clear outline! We need a fresh devotion to the Word become flesh, that His gift to make the people hear Him gladly may become ours. I would tarry with any man in prayer to ask for this grace, but my belief is that it comes sooner by way of work.

Let us pray for the language of sympathy. You listen to a man in the pulpit and sometimes wonder if he has ever been in love, or lost a friend, or had his heart broken. He talks like a machine, grinding out his doctrine and setting forth his ethical propositions. But there is nothing about the forgiveness of God or the saving grace of Jesus Christ. He needs another tongue.

It would be a great thing if the lost language of wonder and awe could be restored to us. So much of our preaching is prosaic, academic, and about as thrilling as the minutes of the last meeting of the PTA. People need to be aroused to the wonder of the Incarnation and shaken up by the audacity of the Christian claim. How to get excitement back into our preaching and bring God's drama back into our drab living— that is the question. Would that we might wait on the Holy Spirit for this precious gift!

I tried to say these things to the fellow I was telling you about at the beginning. But he seemed to grow more discouraged the longer I talked. I got the impression that he considered learning to talk in my tongues harder work than learning to talk in his.

# 9: *Meetings*

I never cease to marvel at the number of meetings people will attend. That anyone would ever go to any gathering which did not demand his presence is more than I can understand. The sweetest sentence in the English language is "I'm not going."

There was a time when I thought it was necessary to attend every meeting in the church and the community. The service club luncheon found me eating the worst lunch of the week every Friday. I am glad, however, that I never did get so low down as to keep perfect attendance for a year. If there was a committee of the chamber of commerce or the community chest, they could count on me. If the women's guild needed an invocation or a benediction, I was their boy. No banquet was complete without the pastor of Central Church at the head table.

Now all this brought great satisfaction to the deacons. They said it was good to have a preacher who was community-minded. They thought it did the church a lot of good to be represented in all sorts of affairs. One fellow became quite put out with me because I refused to go out on Saturday night, since I was out every other night. And it seemed to me that my ministry was a success because I was going about—not necessarily going good, but going about.

One day it came to me that enough was enough. All of a sudden the thought of another luncheon made me ill. To contemplate another long committee meeting out of which nothing would come drove me into a state of melancholia. To watch the precious minutes fly while some well-meaning but not very bright chairman fumbled around appeared an ordeal I could no longer endure. In modern parlance, I had had it.

Then a strange thing took place. I quit going to meetings. Politely but firmly, I swore off. There were times when the old habit nearly conquered me, but if you will forgive what may sound like boasting, I fought it bravely. And I won!

Now comes the strangest thing of all. It really did not seem to matter very much to the community or to the church. There were others who took my place. There were substitutes on every hand, and the meetings continued on the same level. My church went forward as before without any noticeable falling off of the congregation or loss of personal prestige. When I checked up on the meetings I no longer attended, I found, as expected, that hardly ever had I missed anything.

Oh, I still get caught once in a while, in spite of all my efforts. But one learns to smell boredom from afar and run in the other direction. A fellow discovers all kinds of ways to sneak out when the wind is dry and hot, with no promise of rain. One flees instinctively from panel discussions, buzz sessions, and sharing experiences. And in his own study, or his own home, or with a friend, he lets God restore him to sanity. The Gospel is meeting—but on the peril of your soul, never add an *s* to what the Gospel is.

Tommy Harrell

# 10: *Specialization*

Some time ago, an army lieutenant won the national modern pentathlon title at San Antonio. At the end of the meet he had scored the most points in horseback riding, swimming, cross-country, pistol shooting, and fencing. But—get this—he did not win a single event.

Now it seems to me that the ministry is a kind of pentathlon, or more likely a decathlon. Ask any layman what he expects from his preacher, and with a little encouragement he will give you a list as long as your arm. He wants a pastor, a friend, a prophet, a public relations expert, a business genius, an educator, an administrator. And he wants all this for less money than he pays his night watchman. I need not go into what he expects of the preacher's wife and children.

Brethren, we might as well confess that we are not up to it. We cannot win first place in all these events, for God never made His servants such paragons of virtue and ability. Real churchmen know this and stop the childish custom of crying for the moon. They take us for what we are and do the best they can to appreciate us whenever we give our best. Every preacher knows what it means to have those wonderful men and women in the congregation and on the board who hold him up on his weak side. There is more joy in the parsonage over one such person than over a hundred self-appointed pious critics.

But there is a point here that the ministry needs to face. We will not win all the events, but we may win the meet. It is not for us to train for just one phase of our work and take pride in being a first-place contender in one place only. We have too many striving to become single-event champions. Here is a fellow who can preach with grace and power, but he will not visit from house to house, nor will he recognize that the church is something besides a pulpit. Another brother is a good pastor, but on Sunday morning brings shame to anyone with an IQ over 80. We have men who after forty years have not learned that two plus two are four and yet speak their feeble words in every meeting of the finance committee.

Part of the trouble is that we do only what we like to do and we simply refuse to learn tasks we find unpleasant. Today we can usually find some psychological jargon to explain our failure, but the real truth is, we lack discipline. Who likes to deal with church finances? You do? God bless you, brother, for I despise it. But if you will help me to grasp some plain principles, I will try and help you to improve those poor sermons. Maybe John will tell us how he developed a successful educational program.

As I look out across the Church, I see here and there a star in some particular field. But I do not see many of them, and there are never enough to go around. Yet I see more fellows who are good all-around men, and no church fails to grow under their ministry. They have learned to be competent in all phases of their work, but I doubt if they will ever win first prize in any single event. They are "good ministers of Jesus Christ."

Finally, the fellow with only one string to his bow gets a little tiresome both to himself and to others. It may be an age of specialization, but life refuses to become specialized. Living is a pretty wide affair, and the ministry deals with living. Here's to the preachers who win the pentathlon!

# 11. *Jumps*

Lloyd George once remarked that the most dangerous feat in the world is to attempt crossing a chasm in two jumps. To which another man replied that if you could only jump fifteeen feet and the chasm was a hundred feet across, one jump was hardly a safe endeavor, either. In that case, he suggested, it would be better not to jump at all, but walk down and then climb up the other side one step at a time. It strikes me that here we have some valuable insights into church administration.

For one thing, Lloyd George was certainly right in suggesting that some things do not allow a pause in the middle. It has to be done in one jump or it will not go through at all. Do not fire the choir director unless it can be done in one quick operation and made final before the rumors start. Brethren, do not even contemplate hiring a new janitor if you cannot handle it with despatch. Just endure the old one and pray for patience.

It is hardly ever a good idea to announce that you are going to do something unpleasant some time in the future. If it is right, and if it has to be done, let it be over with one leap. This does not mean that you will escape all adverse criticism, but it is much easier to face it with an accomplished fact than with a future probability.

If yours is the responsibility and the authority, make a decision sharp and clear. I followed a man one time who was the most loved man I ever knew. No one spoke of him critically except to suggest that he put off making decisions. Ah, there was the rub! What a situation his successor had to face! He had assumed, apparently, that nothing would blow up until he was out of range. What wonderful opportunities had been passed because the rubbish of unresolved problems blocked the way. May the good Lord save you from loved and indecisive predecessors!

But not all the chasms can be jumped in one leap. We are not strong enough to make it, and woe to the man who has not learned to measure his ability accurately. He will not only fail to get across, but he will get hurt. If there is any question about it, be cautious. Walk down to the bottom and visit with the folks along the way. Then start climbing up the other side, and do not be in too much of a hurry. It is bad on your heart and it makes the people nervous.

The Church is full of good men who attempt thirty-foot leaps with fifteen-foot ability. Because the Church moves slowly, a man is under the temptation to hurry it along. It does take great patience to spend a year on a problem that should be solved in an hour. But speed may postpone a solution forever. Sometimes easy does it.

Do not try to change the order of worship the first Sunday. Do not move the pulpit the second Sunday. Wait until the worship committee recommends changes on a trial basis and then consent to go along with the experiment. Do not push old brother Brown out of five of his eight chairmanships until the nominating committee wants to take the responsibility. Do not let the church get into the habit of saying no, and make sure that enough time has been spent in getting majority support before submitting your plan. This is not politics. Heaven forbid! It is just deciding when to jump and when to walk.

# 12: *Local*

No church is free from bureaucracy, though some are worse than others. But we cannot operate efficiently without the brethren in the "detached" jobs. They are not just necessary evils, but servants of Christ who perform important and central tasks. I have remarkably little prejudice against them, and compared with my attitude in younger days my growth in grace has been considerable.

But when I go to big conferences and hear some pip-squeak refer condescendingly to the "local church," all my youthful ire returns and I have to be restrained. I think of some hard-working, underpaid pastor doing the actual work of the Kingdom while this soft brother-in-Christ spins out his theories and sends out his mimeographed letters. I want to thunder forth denunciations and anathemas on all bureaucrats who forget the rock from which they are hewn. I want to shout: "Without the local church you have neither status nor dignity, for you are the servant of every local pastor! When it comes to being of value to the Church, you can be replaced ten to one over the pastor who preaches every Sunday to his people and shepherds his flock."

Nothing is any good until it is localized, which is the deep meaning of the Incarnation. It was not in the priestly circle at Jerusalem that God revealed Himself, but in a baby in Bethlehem, in a young carpenter in Nazareth, in a weary pilgrim on the Cross. And today He comes to men where they meet on the street and confronts them face to face and not from afar off. For good or ill, it is the local church and the local preacher.

Somebody—probably Chesterton—once remarked that nothing is real until it is local. The national assemblies, the general conferences, have their place; and it not an unimportant one either. The general secretaries, the clerks, the administrators, all have their legitimate functions in the Church's life. But until the resolutions, the plans, and the pronouncements get incarnated on Main Street, they drift like fog before the morning sun and are about as substantial. The battle, dear friends, is won or lost in that local church so despised by some of the Church's proud traveling salesmen.

An educational system has to be administered, and it employes any number of people who never get within a mile of the young people themselves. They, too, serve a great cause, though I have a suspicion that most school systems are overloaded with assistants and associates. But let no one ever forget that education, if it happens at all, takes place in a classroom under the direction of a person called a teacher. All the rest is support.

One of the most serious handicaps the ecumenical movement labors under is discovered when it gets down to the local situation. There it is not the First Ecumenical Church of Podunk we find, but the Episcopal, the Nazarene, the Lutheran Church. Surely those of us who believe in ecumenicity must labor harder to give our vision a local habitation and a name.

I met a fellow the other day who was offered a high-paying national Church secretaryship. He turned it down, and I asked him why. "Because," he replied, "I would rather be concrete than abstract." Ah, yes! Wasn't there a philosopher who wrote about the principle of "concretion"? One of the best illustrations of the principle is a local congregation. So let us have no more of this looking down our noses at the local church, for it alone is the Church.

# 13: *Discussion*

I saw in a well-known preachers' magazine that a fellow says that laymen do not always understand what the preacher says. Shucks! There is nothing new about that, for people do not even understand what they read in the newspapers or hear on the radio. If we are talking about anything more complicated than the time and place of the next church supper, we will be misunderstood. Words mean such different things to different people.

But this professor has a solution. He says we ought to meet right after the sermon and have a discussion group. Then those who are interested could ask questions and offer criticisms. They could pry into that figure of speech flung out in the heat of delivery, and challenge the evidence for that dramatic affirmation. Then everybody could go home to Sunday dinner knowing exactly what the preacher said and filled with peace of mind.

It sounds dandy; except that when I get through preaching I do not want to discuss anything with anybody. I feel badly enough about it, and my physical and spiritual exhaustion makes it difficult to remember my own name or to say a kind word to my wife. I knew an old preacher who slipped out the side door at the close of the service and went home. The people sometimes objected, but if I followed my inclination that would be my procedure. To put the discussion later in the week would just make it another meeting to promote, and I am afraid that most of my parishioners would rather stay home and be unenlightened than meet me at the church.

I got to thinking of what might have happened if Amos's congregation had demanded such a meeting. It might have gone something like this.

LAYMAN: Doctor, shouldn't the clergy be more careful in using the phrase: Thus saith the Lord?

AMOS: By all means. That's why I remain a layman. And I'm not a doctor.

LAYMAN: I think that when you suggest God says, "I hate, I despise your feasts," you are doing a disservice to the Church.

AMOS: Really? How wonderful. That is what I was hoping for.

LAYMAN: When you say such things as "Hear this word, you cows of Bashan," you are using language unbefitting a gentleman.

AMOS: Right you are, brother. But who said I was a gentleman?

LAYMAN: There is nothing more restful than a solemn worship service. Don't you believe in the liturgical revival?

AMOS: Of course I believe in it. By the way, what is it?

LAYMAN: The Church is to help people. When you say, "Woe to you who desire the day of the Lord . . . It is darkness, and not light," you upset the people and take away their comfort.

AMOS: Hurrah! That was the whole idea.

LAYMAN: I do not come to church to hear the preacher talk about such things as injustice, the rich robbing the poor, and God's anger. I want a more positive message.

AMOS: The Jewish Science Church meets down on the next corner.

LAYMAN: The trouble with your sermons is that they have no solutions.

AMOS: Wait a minute, brother. Remember my closing words this morning? "But let justice roll down like waters, and righteousness like an everflowing stream." Quite a solution, it seems to me.

Perhaps the problem is not so much an inability to understand as an unwillingness to listen.

## 14: Security

I saw in the papers a while back that a lady in Palo Alto, California, sent a check for one thousand dollars to the United Nations. She said this was what it would cost to build a private fall-out shelter and she believed it was better to strengthen the organization struggling to prevent war. Somehow, in the midst of all the panic and hysterical double talk, this lifted up my old heart. For here is one with the courage of her convictions, and she does more than talk about them. May her tribe increase!

She raises an interesting point. Just where does our security lie? This is not a new question, and you find it being asked more than once in the Bible. Remember the words of the psalmist?

> *I lift up my eyes to the hills.*
> *From whence does my help come?*
> *My help comes from the Lord,*
> *who made   heaven and earth.*
>                           Psalm 121:1-2

Or there is Isaiah (never mind which one) saying,

> *Woe to those who go down to Egypt for help*
> *and rely on horses,*
> *who trust in chariots because they are many*
> *and in horsemen because they are very strong,*
> *but do not look to the Holy One of Israel*
> *or consult the Lord!*
>                           Isaiah 31:1

And today we have a brave and forthright lady who says, "Others may take refuge in shelters and rely on concrete. But I will trust in man's common sense and hope for peace through debate and co-operation." I tell you, it is wonderful.

27

Without carrying it too far—for analogies are mighty tricky things—we are forever faced with the necessity of deciding between digging a hole in the ground or going out to talk with our neighbors. The hole-diggers are usually regarded as the realists. Their spirit is "Don't trust nobody, but get back into your cave and club the first fellow who tries to share it." You may turn out not to be of much account, but at least you will survive—maybe.

The ones who want to stay out in the open and talk about mutual problems are regarded as the idealists or the dreamers. Why, anybody knows that we are fine folks—all others are selfish and some of them are homicidal maniacs! But these intrepid souls believe that all progress is through growth in co-operation, and they assume there is a common desire to live and not die. So they keep on through all the quarrels, the delays, the broken hopes. All men are brothers, they affirm, and they were meant to walk the earth, feel the sun, breathe fresh air, drink pure water. They will believe in man and not run for the basement because all men are sinners.

Where does God come into this choice? He comes in when we bet our lives that humanity is His creation and human destiny is in His hand. He comes in when we assume that we were not meant to live like moles in a hole or like bats in a cave. God is there whenever we decide not to put all our energy into trying to survive a war rather than trying to eliminate it. How fine it would be if preachers and their churches would make as clear a witness for their faith in the reality of God as that California lady has made for the United Nations.

How about sending a check to your mission board or to the Commission on Christian Social Concerns? If it does not make the papers, I will venture that it gets recorded in the Lamb's Book of Life.

# 15: *Organization Men*

There was an election one time that fooled nearly everybody, including me. The big newspapers were all for the incumbent and they lambasted his opponent day after day until one expected the poor fellow to surrender to the police any day. But gradually my sneaky mind began to get suspicious. Nobody could be that bad. and one day I met this poor candidate. His ideas were a lot like mine and his record looked mighty good to me. When on election day he won, it became obvious that some other people had felt the same way. My point is that when they start to kick a fellow too often and too hard, we had better take a look at who is kicking and why.

Now all of this leads me to raise the question of the "organization man." Wasn't there a book by that title? He is the poor sod who fits into the institution and becomes a cog in the machinery. He never rebels or gets temperamental, and he never comes up with a brilliant inspiration. He just serves the company and is loyal to it according to his ability. He is not admired by the intelligentsia, nor by the critics of American life. Indeed, he is regarded as a kind of disease, and when we grow weary of berating Khrushchev, we pick on him as the cause of our trouble. I tell you it is no compliment to be called an organization man.

Well, I suppose there must be reason for all this antipathy. A man ought to assert himself and be aware of his individuality. He ought to have a higher aim in life than just to hold his place. But there are a lot of pretty good men who are short on inspiration and lacking in leadership ability. The Christian Church never found many St. Pauls, but it had a considerable number of the ones not very wise nor very powerful. They could not write epistles or argue on Mars Hill, but they gave their bodies to be burned, and they did not offer incense before the emperor's statue. You might say that they were just organization men.

Have you ever been responsible for a church or a synod, or a reform movement? Have you ever presided over a college faculty or been (the good Lord forbid) dean of a theological school? If you say yes to any of these questions, I will wager my moth-eaten Cruden's *Concordance* against a 1929 almanac that you have a new appreciation for organization men. They never say it must be their way or they will not play. They take their responsibilities seriously, and you can depend on them to chair a committee or speak to a man about his pledge. They do not regard it as beneath their dignity not to sit at the head table.

And when it comes to the churches, how could we ever survive without these fellows. They are in their places whether they like the preacher or not. The decision to move and build a new church seems like madness to them, but they will go along with the majority vote and will pledge generously to the new enterprise. They may think that some of their church's literature is poor stuff, but they will never insist, therefore, that it is subversive. They do not attend meetings to upset programs or plans, but to listen, vote, and serve. Sometimes these men are called churchmen, and they gladden the preacher's heart.

The mavericks sometimes get the headlines, but the work is usually done by the men who stay in line and put something above their own whims. Jesus had to deal with some prima donnas, but when he saved them, they became the servants of all. Amen!

# 16: *Spectacles*

Sam Spiegel, who produced the movie *Lawrence of Arabia,* has a reputation for being able to stretch a dollar about as far as it will go. "I'll spend money to enhance the drama of a film," he said, "but never to create meaningless spectacle." It came to me suddenly that what was wrong with so many modern films is that they do not heighten drama but merely create spectacles with no meaning. Then I began to think about the Church and preachers.

What has sometimes been called the "Hollywood" influence in modern worship is really this tendency to mistake spectacle for drama. I went through a new church the other day and the minister showed me everything—and I mean everything. From the boiler room, past the air-conditioning machinery, then on to the rest rooms we plodded wearily. Next I went through every single room in the church school unit, and finally arrived at the sanctuary.

The thing this brother wanted me to appreciate most of all, however, was an intricate lighting system which he could control from the pulpit. He could dim the lights or change their color. He could illuminate the cross or cast it in shadow. He could fill the whole place with blinding white light or create that dim, murky atmosphere which Sinclair Lewis once described as characteristic of saloons and churches. But I do not know how a fellow could operate the switchboard without a course in electronics. If this is the trend, then theological seminaries will be forced to train men for electrical engineering and no church will want a man without asking, "How is he as a lights operator?"

I think of the plain New England meeting houses with their clean lines and their simple beauty. Their services were conducted in the light of the sun coming through their windows. The people prayed, sang hymns, and listened to the sermon without any external stage effects. This was the house of God and not a theater.

Ah, but we live in a different day, you say. Quite so! But to people dazzled by flashing neon signs and surrounded by buildings resembling glass boxes, it may be even more striking to be brought into a large quiet room where attention is not centered on lights going up and down. Maybe a calm atmosphere where all eyes are drawn to a cross and an altar will impress them more than a replica of the sights along the Strip at Las Vegas.

And when it comes to preaching, let us learn once and for all that the spectacular style turns the Gospel into melodrama. The magic is not in men or their presentations, nor is it in some startling surprise produced by a flamboyant delivery. The drama, brethren, is in the Word. Never trust the man referred to by worldly people as a "dramatic preacher," for such a man is only a spectacle. When the Gospel is truly preached it is intrinsically exciting.

The effect of what has been made emotionally titillating by external tricks soon wears off, and the victim's latter state is worse than his first. True worship and real preaching not only moves the person; it changes him. Come to think of it, perhaps a fundamental weakness of modern Christianity is a tendency on the part of its professional leaders to mistake spectacle for drama. And, as always, I speak this primarily to my own heart.

# 17: *Rebels*

It is an unusual preacher's magazine that does not carry in about every other issue an article about how church organizations cabin and confine the idealism of young men in the ministry. Sometimes the authors just talk in generalities, but now and then they come right out and say who is to blame. I saw in a homiletical journal the other day that a young Methodist theological student from Texas says that the villains in his church are district superintendents and bishops. I tell you, it is enough to make your blood boil at the way church officials and bureaucrats discourage these boys!

For if anyone has doubts about this criminal situation, let him remember the early years of his own ministry. Fresh from the classroom, we had ideas and ideals. Just like Johnny Yuma on television and in the jukeboxes, we were rebels. Tell us we can't smoke, will they! Mack, pass me that ash tray. They say we have to do it their way, do they? We won't do it at all rather then endure such slavery. Accept the authority of such incompetents? We'd rather be dead. Ah, what wonderful days they were—how brave was our spirit and how limited our experience!

But make no mistake about it, the church which will not listen to its youth will die. For God can say some things to young men that old men cannot hear. Give me the boy with energy and the spirit of adventure, any day. He will fall on his face and he may antagonize the old-timers, but wherever there is life there is hope. May the good Lord deliver us from the young fogies who are harness-broken before they have a chance to kick up their heels! Treat the rebels kindly, O Church Fathers, and give them love and appreciation.

Now, so far as the young men themselves are concerned, there is

33

not much an older man can say to them that they will hear, let alone understand. This is the curse that life puts on parents, teachers, and people over forty. You are disqualified automatically, and if you are a church official with any authority over the probationers, may the Lord help you to speak softly and patiently. For sometimes the youngsters are right, and you have grown too timid, too cautious, with too little sense of adventure remaining in your soul.

Yet I must put down a conclusion which comes out of some years of association with board secretaries, standing committee chairmen, moderators, and bishops. When these men resist young ministerial ideals, usually it is because they have found that these particular ones won't work. These old boys may be a little short on enthusiasm but they are often mighty long on wisdom. Often they love the Lord and the people with their whole hearts. Among them are to be found the rare elders who foverer remain young in heart. I am not willing yet to lump them all together as the enemies of young and fearless prophets.

You will hardly ever find a fellow, either young or old, who thinks that all is right with the Church. Not many of them think that all is right with their own lives. If you have a new insight or a fresh word, there are still a good many people who will recognize the authentic thing when it appears. And if at times you rebel at being a part of a team or a system—well, there are mighty few situations in life where you can play the part of the Lone Ranger. Infiltrate, son, and see how much easier it is to win acceptance of creative and daring leadership than you thought. Thus endeth the lesson.

# 18: *Educators*

There is a trend in homiletic discussion to lean heavily on educators for guidance and light. Articles on preaching appear, in what seem to me increasing numbers, from professors of psychology, ethics, history, and culture. I have been helped by all these brethren when they talk about their own specialties, and all these fields of knowledge are important for the preacher's art. But when they start pronouncing what is wrong with preaching, they fall flat on their faces because they know precious little about it. I am not opposed to educators. Why, some of my best friends are educators. But oh, what a world of difference there is between preaching and teaching!

The main difference is that preaching always contains the element of proclamation and teaching does not. The preacher is aware of an event, and he has been captured by an experience. He is not sent forth primarily to offer it as an option—at least not in his role as preacher. He is commissioned to proclaim it. He is the "babbler" on Mars Hill, telling his strange story in the midst of philosophers and the sophisticated. His word is of something that has happened, and he speaks of the action of God.

There was a time when seminaries were so full of the spirit of the time that they tried to turn religion into science. The scientific method was to be our method and the scientific spirit was to be our spirit. I could go along with it part of the way, but on Sunday morning when I stood in the pulpit of my student church, I knew the whole thing was nonsense. I was not there to say "maybe"—I was there to say, "I know whom I have believed." I was to proclaim the Good News that God has provided for us power to live by and power to become the children of God.

Now, professors of other disciplines besides theology can help us poor preachers very much. They can teach us history, and Christianity is an historical religion. They can teach us to speak plainly and enunciate clearly. They can tell us much about the contemporary mind and the contemporary viewpoint. They can give us psychological principles which will help us understand why Mrs. Jones is so ornery and why old man Smith is so bitter. But when it comes to what constitutes the heart of preaching, they know very little about it. Let them know their limitations and not try to give advice to the man called by God to be a witness of His grace, for they are really not able.

All is not well with preaching. Try and find a real preacher and see how few there are. Even the ones who can speak gracefully and acceptably are often lacking in power. They seem to have been studying the wrong kind of theology; much of the stuff coming out of modern pulpits seems to have lost the main point somewhere. There is a vague sense of something missing throughout the churches, and I am not trying to say that preaching does not need help. But it will not be forthcoming from the departments of education in the universities or the graduate schools of theology.

Maybe we can get it from the Apostle Paul, or from Francis Asbury, or Billy Graham, or the Salvation Army. Ultimately, of course, we must receive the baptism of the Holy Spirit, which does not come to us easily or according to our command. We will have made some small progress toward the revival of preaching, however, if we know where not to look. Editors: Please take note!

# 19: *Harmless*

You may have heard of the old Scotch lady who referred to a young man as obviously fitted for the ministry because he was "a right harmless laddie." I do not know of a more devastating thing to say about preachers and pastors. Call them egotists, for many of us are. Refer to them as trouble-makers, since many of us must plead guilty to that charge. Brand them as men lacking proper respect for the successful and powerful, for this is an attitude that breaks above the surface every now and then. But may the good Lord forbid that any man looking at us should say: "Harmless!"

Yet for many a layman this is the picture of the ideal minister. He must be "spiritual," by which he means otherworldly. He must be willing to run errands and do whatever the church cannot get anybody else to do. He must speak of matters so esoteric and general that no man will be stabbed in his conscience or troubled in his mind. Let preachers believe that all is well, while the practical men go on about their business. The minister cannot do any harm at a wedding or a funeral, and if he can tell some pretty good stories after dinner for free, that will be fine.

But even sadder than this distorted picture held by some laymen is the image too many preachers have of themselves. We begin to think of ourselves as "right harmless laddies." I have listened to cheap entertainment by preachers, priests, and rabbis who have long ago lost all sense of speaking for God and to men. Having eased the tension of discipline, they become commercial men with one eye on profit and the other on safety. Jerome gave us the right word for such creatures: "Shun, as you would the plague, a cleric who from being poor has become wealthy, or who, from being a nobody has become a celebrity." Let all the people respond, "Amen!"

Now the New Testament has a great respect and fear of the Word. It has no comfort for the preachers whose cozy little talks pass for sermons. The Bible never thought of religion as harmless. Listen to Hebrews (4:12-13): "For the word of God is living and active, sharper than any two-edged sword, piercing to the division of soul and spirit, of joints and marrow, and discerning the thoughts and intentions of the heart. And before him no creature is hidden, but all are open and laid bare to the eyes of him with whom we have to do." Until a man recognizes that he is dealing with something that can turn the world upside down, he is not worthy of the Christian ministry.

A doctor reports that when he was an assistant to a great professor of therapeutics, he heard him say many times, "If you are told that a medicine is harmless, you may take it that it also lacks any healing properties." And that is a good word for a drug-addicted generation. All the talk about all the medicines and pills that can cure you without any danger of hurting you is false. To study medicine is to learn how to take calculated risks.

It is sad news for the boys who are only comfort-dispensers to learn that too much comfort can destroy a man. If what I say next Sunday morning cannot possibly hurt anyone, it cannot help anyone either. Remember, we wield a two-edged sword with sharp edges. We are not little boys playing with wooden ones.

# 20: *Payrolls*

Whenever a layman wants to put a preacher in his place or discount his message, he is likely to say, "He never met a payroll." That is supposed to take care of the whole matter by proving that the preacher is an idealistic, otherworldly, impractical dreamer. The implication seems to be that only a man running a business is qualified to speak on matters of social significance. Sometimes a fellow feels like urging our theological seminaries to put in a course at once on "How To Meet a Payroll."

Of course, you could make a pretty good case for the idea that the man who is embroiled in business affairs is the last one to decide rules and regulations for the good society. I would hate to have some bankers I have known decide how much to spend for education. It would be disastrous for some manufacturers to tell us how much we should allow for slum clearance. It is easy for men whose chief goal is profits to see no further and be concerned with nothing more. Some of the payroll-meeters have such limited interests that culture would die if it depended on them.

But I feel in a generous mood today and am quite willing to consider the preacher and his relation to payrolls. The first thing that comes to my mind is the number of opportunities the Church has missed because practical laymen were blind. The preacher pleaded in vain for a new sanctuary or a new educational building to serve better a community that was growing. Then some dear old corporation president remembered that his children had been baptized in the old church, and with sentimental tears shining in his hard eyes he blocked the whole plan.

Where does the church budget come from, and who pays the

janitor's salary? Who gets the credit if the budget is oversubscribed? The campaign chairman! Who gets the blame if it is undersubscribed? The preacher! Upon whose shoulders rests the responsibility of inspiring people to give cheerfully and generously? Where does the missionary enterprise get its support, and where do the dollars come from to pay for the religious education of our youth? I tell you, brethren, when you think of the money raised by churches under the leadership of pastors who "never met a payroll," it is a miracle. Also, it makes some of the monetary affairs of some laymen look like peanuts.

What we could say about ministers who give to every good cause and send their children to college on six thousand a year! It is impossible—but they go right on doing it. Now and then a preacher borrows and never pays his debts. But these are rare birds and finally fly the ecclesiastical coop. Most of them—nay, 99.99 per cent of them—pay their bills, dress their wives decently if not lavishly, and manage to produce the most useful citizens in their communities.

The next time somebody says that preachers do not meet payrolls, let us say to him kindly but firmly, "Brother, most preachers meet more payrolls in a month than most men meet in a year. And they do it by persuading reluctant church members to give in spite of a dozen eloquent reasons they present to prove they cannot afford it. Oh yes, and they must do it without making them mad." Let us stand for the benediction!

## 21: *Criticism*

I was walking along the other day with nothing much on my mind (a not unusual situation), when I ran into an old friend. He is pastor of a little church out in the country near a little town called River Center. He seemed disturbed about something, and his usually leisurely manner was somewhat agitated. "Got a minute?" he asked abruptly. We found a coffeehouse and an empty table. I have found sometimes that a cup of good coffee and a fifteen-minute break with a friend is better than an hour on the couch. "Shoot!" I said, which is a little too abrupt and directive according to the latest books, but as I said, we were old friends.

"You ever notice," he began, "how many fellows are sounding off like experts who don't know what they are talking about?"

"Sure," I replied, "It has always been that way. Today, with so many guys a long way from home, we just have more experts, that's all."

"Don't be smart with me," he snapped. "I'm older than you, and smarter too. You city fellows get a lingo that makes some people think you are clever. I know better." I apologized meekly.

"What I mean," he said, "is that the ministry is being defined, criticized, analysed, pitied, generalized, by people who never were ministers."

He had my interest now. "Elucidate," I commanded.

"Well," he went on, "here's an article in a preacher's magazine by a dean of a theological seminary. Now this fellow has never been out of a classroom. He never served a student church. He never had to deal with an ornery music committee or resist the lethargy of the deacons. You know what he says about ministers? He says they are arrogant and full of pride. I don't know anybody like that—except you," he added nastily. I ignored it and he went on.

41

Tommy Harrell

"Another fellow writes that we are all promoters who have lost our sense of spiritual mission. You know who he is? A church bureaucrat who served a student church for one year. That was all the people could stand. Now there comes along a retired candy manufacturer who says the ministers are Communist dupes. I tell you, I've had about all I can take."

He paused a moment, but before I could get a word in he was off again. "Now, preachers have all sorts of faults. Some of us are lazy and some of us don't shine our shoes. But the fellows I know are running themselves ragged trying to help people. When a community gets hysterical, it's usually a preacher who stands up and gets thrown at. Ever hear of ecclesiastical freedom riders? We stamp out more communism in a minute than all these delayed adolescents playing spy will find in a hundred years. We try to tell the kids something about God and our Lord on Sunday while their parents are filling them with TV swill all the rest of the week. We're not as bright or inspiring as we ought to be. But please, let's have an end to these smart remarks from people who never sat up all night with the husband of a dying wife and never had to tell a mother her boy was killed in an accident."

For once in my life I had nothing to say, and God gave me sense enough to keep quiet. I waited. He finished his coffee.

"Thanks for the coffee," he grinned, and was on his way.

I thought about all the preachers I know and I got agitated, too. Who writes all this stuff anyway? Not the fellow who is bearing the burden of the day. He is too busy trying to move his congregation along another inch here and prevent a backwash there. Let these experts learn the glory and tragedy of being a pastor before they pontificate.

## 22: *Informality*

I always shudder when a fellow gets up in a meeting and says he will not take time to read his report but will only "lift up a few highlights." The expression itself bothers me, for lifting up highlights is too much for my imagination. But worse than the mixed figure of speech is the practical certainty that this procedure will take more time, lack balance, and be generally dull. For such presentations have had little preparation, and in the name of being more informal they usually are less effective. Not a man in a million can measure time when he is on his feet speaking without careful organization of his remarks.

If these informal brethren could be confined to business meetings, which are seldom of ultimate importance anyway, the harm would not be great. But they are called to pastorates and ordained to conduct public worship. They seldom go through a service without the necessity of calling the janitor or an usher to the pulpit to receive some new signals which the brother just decided on. They come out with homey little remarks which seldom fit and never deepen the congregation's sense of the presence of God. They call out the name of a man in the congregation who broke a hundred in golf yesterday, or they ask a family to stand who is going to Europe next week.

The prayer is so folksy that it makes you embarrassed. It is worse than calling the President of the United States "Jack" on the first presentation. Such men have never sensed the majesty of God, apparently, and their ideas of reverence have been developed at the weekly meetings of the local Lions Club. Ah, but wait until they get to the announcements! Here they take from ten to twenty minutes in commenting on every gathering in the church from choir practice to the high-school basketball game on Friday. One of the players belongs to the young people's society.

The sermon never goes deeper than the silly moralisms of a religious columnist. Faithful friends are likely to say, "At least he meets people where they are." That would not be so bad if he did not get down there where they are and make sure that they stay there. So the congregation becomes a fellowship of mediocrity whose religious insights and understanding remain on the level of the kindergarten.

The alternative is not the Roman Mass nor the Eastern Orthodox liturgy. It is a realization that, if you do not read the prayers or the sermon, you will have to work harder on them than if you did. If you are going to depart from the text, then prepare yourself with fasting and supplication. Free worship is not sloppy worship, and dignity is always the mark of Christians who have gathered to worship God.

It is true that the preacher has to work with what he has. He may have inherited an untrained congregation, and many of his people may have lost their sense of the holiness of the sanctuary. But people, even when they are uneducated and uncultured, respond to quality and soon learn to despise the second-rate. It is the minister's privilege to incarnate the spirit of worship, but it is a costly privilege. Informality will betray us unless we learn that it demands more physical, mental, and spiritual discipline than just reading the report.

## 23 · *Now*

There were those who referred to the early Methodist circuit riders as "Now" men. They came with a promise of something happening now, and they thought it quite possible that a man might have his life changed in a moment. Whether or not God performs instantaneous conversions has been the subject of long and often dull theological debate. But the frontier preachers never had any doubt in this matter. They could not stay and spend a year or more in one place. If they could not expect immediate results from their preaching, they were futile.

Well, there are some instances in the New Testament to suggest that these brethren were right in expecting sudden experiences of salvation. It happened that way to Paul. Of course, there was much back of that moment on the Damascus road, I have no doubt. But the immediate decision was made when he saw a light and heard a voice. Indeed, one of my friends says that the reason the brethren at Jerusalem were suspicious of him was because he had not gone through the membership class. They belonged to the school which keeps a fellow out of the church until he has had the proper training.

There was the incident of Philip and the Ethiopian eunuch. You remember that the Book of Acts tells about a man reading from Isaiah without comprehension. He welcomed Philip's offer to explain it to him. Now the preacher did not explain that, first of all, there are three or maybe four Isaiahs. The story says: "Then Philip opened his mouth, and beginning with this scripture he told him the good news of Jesus" (Acts 8:35). A little later we hear the Ethiopian saying, "See, here is water! What is to prevent my being baptized?" It was done, and Philip was taken away by the Spirit and the Ethiopian went on his way rejoicing.

45

I am aware, brethren, of how essential nurture is and how important it is that men should have training in churchmanship. Let us not minimize these matters, nor let us think we have to make a choice between sudden spiritual happenings and long training. But consider what it would do for our ministry and for the Church if we were to recapture the NOW spirit.

In most of our services any sense of expectancy is lacking. Actually, we do not think much is going to happen; and we are not disappointed. Our Gothic cathedrals, our robed choirs, our educated presentations all create an atmosphere of relaxation and leisureliness. Fine! Our harried spirits are in need of rest. But we are also in need of a new life, a new direction, a new commitment. We are in desperate need of being born again. We need a miracle!

Are we going to turn over this part of the Gospel to the tabernacle? Are we satisfied to leave the invitation to the evangelists? Is there any place for the promise of a mighty, immediate breakthrough to God in our services? Do we hold out any hope that our eyes may be opened now to the presence of the Lord Jesus? I wonder if we are not in great need of learning how to be "Now" men again.

A few years ago, when I was in seminary, much talk in theology centered around the word "crisis." I never objected to this term, for it described the situation I was in most of the time. It is the situation a vast number of people are in right now. They are not drawn to a fellowship which will put them through a training course or outline for them a six-year study. They want someone to tell them how to find God in a hurry. Training and study are all a part of our program, and we shall neglect them at our peril. But can we leave our discussions and our debates long enough to seek an immediate word from the Lord? It is a great thing to have a word for tomorrow. It is wonderful that ours is an eternal message. But boys, what do you have to say about it NOW?

## 24: *Clothes*

Thomas Carlyle was much read in my younger days but I fear he is much neglected by this generation. I doubt that to mention *Sartor Resartus* here will rouse much of an enthusiastic response. It is a pity! You see, this was a book on clothes, and from this starting point Carlyle traveled into the realms of theology, philosophy, history. Strange how stimulated a fellow can get just thinking about what men wear to cover their nakedness and decorate their persons. Of course everybody knows what women make out of this apparel business, but we are talking about men, and for the present about ministers.

Now Jesus advised ". . . do not be anxious, saying, . . . 'What shall we wear?'" (Matt. 6:31) But his servants seem more concerned about this matter than they have in days past. I was at a ministerial meeting the other day and the boys began talking about proper dress. It seemed to me that this subject aroused more interest and caused more discussion than the problem of housing or juvenile delinquency. Indeed, there was a vigorous debate.

One group was quite rude in deriding clerical collars, robes in the pulpit, and other fineries adding color to the man of God. This, they intimated, was popery and a sure sign of the deterioration of the Church. I happened to know that one of the brothers who spoke long on this side of the question had been known to wear tan shoes in the pulpit. His wife gave the clincher when she said that preachers are not to be concerned with such things but "just follow Jesus." But my imagination saw the brethren wearing white robes, sandals, and long hair. I decided hastily that she must not have meant what she said about following Jesus to be taken literally in the matter of apparel.

The more formal brothers spoke of the advantages of round collars.

47

Some had escaped traffic citations, some had been placed at the head of lines, and in one case a fellow had given a clerically attired preacher his seat on a bus. But most of the company seemed to consider these reasons on the frivolous side and turned to weightier arguments.

They said that a minister ought to be distinguishable everywhere. They believed that opportunities of service are opened to such a man which the business-suited preacher will never get. They argued that in an increasingly secular society, ministers do something significant if they are visible symbols of the Church. This point of view made a considerable impression on my mind, as I have lost my confidence in preachers who are mere after-dinner entertainers. The idea that the less a minister is regarded as a "man of God" and the more he is thought of as a "regular guy" the better, has about run its course. The Church and its servants ought to have some distinguishing marks.

Well, the debate ended as the ones Omar Khayyam attended in his youth, when he came out by that same door where in he went. I doubt that any man changed his mind in the slightest, except possibly a certain old preacher who is notoriously unstable. But one man struck a fine concluding note. He said that, whatever we wear outside, he hoped that our souls were clothed in the white robes of those who have come out of the great tribulation and have been washed in the blood of the Lamb. To which it seemed to me that the angels around the throne cried: "Amen!"

# 25 : *Image*

Is there any profession in the world that suffers more than the ministry when it comes to the popular image? I have discussed this with my doctor and lawyer friends, and they tell me they fare no better, but I cannot believe it. At least their detractors pay them the honor of regarding them as men. Preachers so often end up as a kind of third sex.

Long ago I concluded that most of the novels written about ministers are authored by maiden ladies who lived very sheltered lives. The bloodless little Lord Fauntleroys they describe could never have come from anywhere but the Land That Never Was. They must be some female's dream-child, doomed to dwell in a hothouse atmosphere where the flowers smell so sweet they make you sick. If the ministry were made up of these angelic softies, the Church would never have made it into the second century.

It is almost a relief to have somebody write about Elmer Gantry. At least it gets the ministry out of the stratosphere. But as is true of most of us, novelists like Sinclair Lewis go from one extreme to another. In an attempt to make the minister human and a sinner—as indeed he is—they make him an unbelievable caricature of a human being. I do not believe that our characteristic sin is sex, but pride. This is too subtle for the writers aiming at the best-seller list.

Now and again a preacher decides to write about his profession from an autobiographical point of view, although in the form of fiction. But it never fools anybody, in spite of the assumed name. His friends spot it in a hurry, and soon it is common knowledge that he is really so and so, his villains are well-known church officials, and the plot is laid in Nevada. These boys are like the soldiers who swore during the war that someday they would write a book about the Army. Their efforts come under the heading of psychotherapy and fall in the same category as "true confessions."

Well, the Church goes on in spite of all this bad and inadequate press. This is because the ministry has many "simple, honorable men" who offset the flamboyant, the boring, the tasteless. People have sudden tragedies and find in their ministers unexpected depths and sincere sympathy. So when they read novels they remember how their preacher sounded a trumpet in the midst of their despair and how their pastor came to sit with them after the friends and neighbors had gone their own ways. Then all the phonies who linger along the edges of the ministry do very little harm. Once you have seen the real thing, the substitutes are easily spotted.

We are all in this together and every man has a responsibility to the others. Surely there is no fellowship where we are more at the mercy of our colleagues. We have given hostages to one another, and no man ought to do anything or say anything without remembering that he represents a goodly fellowship. Perhaps these three propositions may help us.

1. Let us observe a decent reticence about our personal affairs. We do not have to tell the congregation about every family difficulty, every personal yielding to a temptation, every disappointment, every betrayal. Such things are to be taken to the Lord in prayer.

2. If the church officialdom is out of line, then let us deal with it in the fellowship. After all, we do not parade our family problems down Main Street.

3. Let every minister stand again at the altar where he took his ordination vows and repeat them over every week. For the image gets blurred and soiled when we forget who we are.

# 26: *Football*

Have you ever noticed how some of the most profound insights come from the most unexpected places? Who would expect a football coach to speak wisely about homiletics? But some time ago Hayden Fry, coach at Southern Methodist University, was addressing a luncheon of SMU fans. Said he, "I'm the oratorical equivalent of a blocked punt." What a description of some speeches! What expert sermon criticism!

Now and again you have seen it happen on the football field. The kicker steps back, the signals are called, the ball is snapped. With a particular gracefulness, a booming fifty-yard punt is started on its way. But somebody smothers it, and instead of great achievement the result is consternation and disaster. So it was with last Sunday's sermon. Everything was just right, but somehow it never came off. No yardage was gained, no advance was made. A number of invisible blockers were there before the ball got into the air.

I hate to remember the number of times I have sat in the stands—I mean the congregation—and watched this happen. The fellow had a good team, which appeared to be giving him good suport. The choir director did not wave his hands too much and the choir sang on key. The organist was neither too shrinking nor too aggressive. The associate could read without mumbling or slurring. The ushers did not bring people down to the front during the anthem or the prayer. The custodian did not open a window during the moment of silence and his shoes did not squeak. Everything was going just fine.

Then came the moment for the long kick, and we waited expectantly for a soaring advance. The introduction started rather well. But it began to falter and hesitated until it was obvious that this was all there was going to be to it. A start and an intention, but no launching. Suddenly we knew that our brother had been swarmed over.

One of the main things for a man to learn is that he must get it away in a hurry. Wavering attention, worrying about the monthly payments to the finance company, Johnny's poor marks at school, falling sales, are some of the opponents who will spoil the kick if you do not get it off quickly. They will block a man's punt every time unless he is too fast for them. He will win or lose it in a few seconds. Nothing is much worse than to suggest something in the opening moments "to which we shall return later." That is like telling a fellow that it is a mighty long time until dinner, and his mind automatically blocks the preacher's attempt to create expectancy. These opponents are not malicious or consciously out to ruin you. But brethren, the results are the same as if they were.

Do you remember St. Andrew of Crete's hymn?

> *Christian! dost thou see them*
> *On the holy ground,*
> *How the powers of darkness*
> *Rage thy steps around?*

He knew the facts of the Christian life.

Preacher, dost thou see them? Be on thy guard! They will block your efforts unless you move with despatch and assurance. There is no time for fumbling and indecision. There is no place for banalities or triteness. Get on with it, man, before you are blocked!

# 27: *Dropouts*

An educator was talking to me the other day about some of the problems of school administration. He is an able and good man as well as my friend. He said he was worried about the number of dropouts in his school and thus far had failed to find the answer. On graduation night, he saw the empty chairs of those who had started bravely but were not present to receive their diplomas. They were dropouts, and as any man knows, without education today the future is very gloomy.

Well, this preacher began some serious soul-searching and came up with some disquieting thoughts. How many times and in how many places have I been among the dropouts? Do not press me, for it is bad enough after I have given myself the benefit of every doubt and the advantage of every consideration. I am haunted by all the opportunities the good Lord has given me, and the times I started but grew weary of well-doing. I cannot forget the projects begun which would have made me a better man and a more adequate minister—but I dropped out. There are the times when the cause seemed too unpopular and I looked for a side door. But why go on? It is small comfort that some of you may be as uncomfortable as I am if you follow such dangerous musings.

This sense of guilt will help us be more tolerant in our dealings with the church member dropouts. We take a haughty and superior attitude toward the old revivalists who converted so many and lost them so quickly. There was an excessive leakage, it is true, but I wonder if we are doing much better. How many members do you have to take into your church in order to show a net gain? How often do you "clean up the rolls" and wonder what happened to the people who are no longer there? Why does the modern church enroll so many new members and create so few disciples? Why do we run so fast to stay where we are?

Well, even Jesus lost one of the twelve. Paul had to write sadly, "For Demas, in love with this present world, has deserted me and gone to Thessalonica . . ." (2 Tim. 4:10) In any cause there will be the sunshine soldiers and the summer patriots, as Thomas Paine said. But woe unto us if we fall into the evil habit of dropping out whenever the going gets hard.

We must learn how to help the people who begin with high aims but will lose the vision unless it is held before them. Sometimes it seems to me that the minister is the man who keeps the great consummation ever before his people and keeps alive the sense of how wonderful it is to be on the way. Surely this is an important part of preaching and an essential task for the pastor. A good many of these desertions are to be laid at our door. We let the glory fade and the fellowship become too formal and cold. We fail to ask for sacrifice and devotion, and settle for passive attendance and a check.

A friend of mine bought a small German car, and when I asked him how it worked he said, "Fine, except it has a tendency to ausgepoopen on der hillen." So do you and so do I. But there is One who will help us to help our people all the way. Remember, we signed up for the whole course.

# 28: *Amateurs*

I saw a play the other night put on by amateurs. This in itself is bad enough, for I take a dim view of amateur theatricals. But in this case I had seen the play previously done by a competent professional cast. I tell you, the contrast made it a difficult evening.

Well, a fellow begins to think on such occasions—he has to do something to get away from the stumbling, the dragging, the poor timing, the artificial emotions and false gestures. I began to think about God and His entrusting of the Divine Drama to us amateurs. Of course there was Jesus, whose production was perfect, and there have been some others who played their parts in a very satisfactory and accomplished manner. But for the most part God has to use us fumblers, and it must cost Him constant pain. If we could give Him a competent cast, what an impression the drama would make on the world!

Then I thought of my own poor efforts and found precious little comfort following this line. I know the words all right, and the general plot is clear enough. But when it comes to presenting it to the people, those poor clods on the stage were doing a better job than I do. How inept is my effort and how wooden are my actions. No wonder the people yawn and look at their watches. Why doesn't God ring down the curtain and say, "I've had enough."

I began to think about the greatness of God. It came to me in a new way that His patience is beyond man's comprehension. That men should neglect Him no longer seemed so strange to me, considering the kind of representation we give Him. For it came to me that whenever the Word is clearly presented, men have always listened and responded. The fault is not in the Word but in the preaching of it. Oh, the amazing grace of God that trusts the Word to us!

Then I began to have more sympathy for the actors on the stage. I remembered the sign over the piano in the old saloon: "Don't shoot the piano player. He is doing the best he can." Did I do any better last Sunday in presenting my message than they were doing in trying to get their play across the lights to the people? I am afraid not.

So if God had decided to entrust the treasure to earthen vessels, what shall we do about it? We must certainly do the best we can, for anything less is not to be considered. One of the best things we can do is study the pros. If we sit at the feet of the masters as often as possible, we may get some clues which will markedly improve our work. We ought to listen to the critics, who may tear us apart, but at least have a wide experience and a knowledge of what competence is. We must not despise hard work, and we must not shun perfecting the details.

Then it came to me that if the amateur is not a phony, he often rises above himself. For there was one girl on the stage who so obviously felt deeply the part she was playing that she carried authority. In one scene she came across in great power, for she was living the part. I realized suddenly that this carries more conviction than the smooth, slick performance of some professionals.

So I felt a little better about the whole affair. I even stayed around to thank the girl whose one scene had impressed me. I resolved to keep fresh in my mind the miracle of the drama I was to proclaim to the people. And I prayed that God would make me so aware of the grandeur of the Gospel that I might rise above myself now and then in presenting it.

bar

## 29: *Ecumenicity*

I ran into my old country preacher from River Center the other day. We had not seen each other for a long time, and to my query, "What have you been doing lately?" he replied, "Attending an ecumenical consultation. Care to hear about it?"

"No," I answered instinctively. But then I thought better of it and apologized. Besides, my old friend is never dull, mainly because he says what he thinks. So we found us a table, and over coffee and doughnuts we talked about the meeting.

"I'll begin with the good stuff first," he said. "The worship services were fine because they showed me something different. There was an Eastern Orthodox priest who conducted them, and I'll tell you one thing, chum, he made me feel like I was in the presence of God. Of course," he added hastily, "it wouldn't go at River Center, but it helped me; it fed my soul.

"Then," he said, "I liked meeting all those other fellows from other churches. Some of them were mighty kind to an old country preacher and a few of them seemed interested in hearing about my work. A couple of them were disappointed in my lack of problems or, as they called them, 'frustrations.' Yet I got to do my share of talking.

"But when they started to discuss the obstacles to ecumenicity, they left me, and from then on it sounded like the minutes of a ministerial association meeting of a hundred years ago. Those were the days when they wondered if anybody but Baptists could be saved, or if anybody but Methodists were orthodox. But the preachers I know haven't been thinking that way for a long time. Let me tell you what I mean.

"There was a fellow who began to talk about what he called apostolic succession. Near as I could make out, he thought that unless you were ordained by the right bishop you were not really a minister. Now that is just stupid, because some of the greatest preachers in the world were not ordained by any kind of bishop. But this fellow wouldn't drop it, and I got awful tired of having him bring it into every discussion.

"Then there was a brother who wanted to be sure we have the right definition of the church. I rather liked what he had to say until he began insinuating that any church not like his was neither healthy nor whole. Shucks! We are bound to have different ideas of churches, but what good does it do to say that mine is healthy and yours is sick? My guess is that we are all sick sometimes.

"I got to thinking. Some of us have been working together for years and respecting each other for years. It never seemed to me that I ought to draw back from any Christian church, for they have a lot to teach me and mine. I do not object to all kinds of theories about the ministry if they don't call me names. I like to talk with men whose theology is different from mine, and it is clear enough that my ideas are one-sided and my church is not the one and only. Why all this fuss?

"Do you suppose," he asked, "that some of these ecumenical spokesmen ought to keep quiet and stay home until they have arrived at the point an old country preacher reached years ago?"

He was on his feet abruptly as was his custom and headed for the door. "Thanks for the coffee," he called over his shoulder. "The lecture was worth that much."

And I allowed it was.

# 30: *Routine*

I was a little shocked the other day to run across something that Frederick W. Robertson of Brighton had said about preaching. He is one of the great nineteenth-century English preachers whose reputation has grown steadily. Yet in a letter to a friend he wrote: "I wish I did not hate preaching so much, but the degradation of being a Brighton preacher is almost intolerable. . . . Nor am I speaking of the ministeral office; but only the 'stump orator' portion of it—and that I cannot but hold to be thoroughly despicable."

My first reaction is that if hating preaching would give us another Robertson, then may the good Lord destroy our affection for it. I am at a loss to understand just what he meant, but I have the feeling also that something important is involved in his rebellion. Was he suspicious of anything from the pulpit that became popular? Perhaps. Did it trouble him that the Gospel was no longer a stumbling block to the Jew and foolishness to the Greek? Did growing congregations depress his spirit? Or was the hard work involved in preparing and delivering a sermon so burdensome that he found no joy in it? Who can tell!

One thing, however, seems beyond dispute. He took preaching seriously. Nobody hates what he considers unimportant, and it may be that hating a thing is a more honorable reaction than ignoring it. I have read a number of theologians who intimate that God is more pleased with those who actively oppose Him than with those whose actions reveal a feeling that He is dead. I find this idea quite easy to accept, since nothing is more humiliating than a failure to arouse either respect or dislike. Chesterton somewhere pronounces woe upon those who treat God like an old institution. Remember the word addressed to the church at Laodicea: "I know your works: you are neither cold nor hot. Would that you were cold or hot! So, because you are lukewarm, and neither cold nor hot, I will spew you out of my mouth" (Rev. 3:15-16).

The weakness of much of our modern preaching is that those who do it show no sign of either loving it or hating it. The Sunday morning sermon is neither better nor worse than the rest of the routine actions of our professional activities. There is no sign of the weeping Jeremiah cursing the day he was born because of the impossible burden of his calling. There is no intimation that the man in the pulpit has any necessity laid upon him. The performance, in a word, is about as exciting as an academic bore's "on the one hand" alternating with his "but on the other hand, . . ."

Tolerance is often the fruit of doubt. Not always, but often. We are not so sure about a thing as we once were, so we get tolerant all of a sudden. What we bet our lives on is not easy to be tolerant about. Though it is not confessed publicly or even privately, we have grown tolerant of preaching, and that is a terrible mood to be in. I wonder if the time has come for us to pray, "Lord, if I cannot love preaching, help me to hate it. But save me from my present attitude of amiable unconcern."

Brethren, no man should be able to shoulder the obligation of proclaiming the Good News without strong reaction. Run from it if you must, for God can catch Jonah in the middle of the sea. Head toward Damascus if you will, for God in Christ can make Paul hear a voice and see a light. But pray for salvation from the terrifying malady of routine habit. As long as we are in that condition, there is no redemption.

# 31 : Communism

I am not much of a classical scholar, or a scholar of any kind, for that matter. But I was thinking the other day of a word Shakespeare uttered which seems particularly appropriate today. Mark Antony said at Julius Caesar's funeral:

> *The evil that men do lives after them;*
> *The good is oft interred with their bones.*

Ask the Germans if they are quite through with a man named Hitler even though he is dead. Enquire of the Italians whether Mussolini is completely silenced. And then, my countrymen, look about and see if the ghost of McCarthyism does not still roam through our American society.

That evil spirit has a special influence on second-rate preachers and laymen who do not have the ability to win attention to themselves. They are haunted by the possibility of making headlines if they will only attack the churches and the National Council for following what they call "the Communist line."

Now, I am never sure what the so-called Communist line is supposed to be. But this accusation is made against those who are opposed to some of the bizarre and stupid procedures of the House Un-American Activities Committee. It is a label pasted on men who want a change in our immigration policies or think we ought to discuss the relation of Red China to the rest of the world. It has become a general attempt to smear issues without being forced to analyze them or discuss them.

But what is the Communist line? It wavers, twists, turns, contradicts itself, reverses itself overnight, and regards black as white if there seems to be any immediate profit in it. Russian economics are adjusted to any situation and Russian politics are notoriously without principle. By its very nature, communism assumes that propaganda is more important than truth.

But one line which communism follows and never turns aside from is a determination to destroy religion and the churches by any method available. It may tolerate the Church when it must, but it will destroy it when it can. From the time when Karl Marx announced: "Religion . . . is the opiate of the people," his followers have never wavered from their conviction that until Christianity is dead, they are not safe.

So the one sure sign of the follower of the Communist line is an attempt to sow distrust and suspicion among members and supporters of the churches. These are the boys we had better investigate. I had a letter the other day from a fellow who attacked the National Council of Churches. I wrote back and said that since his approach was so obviously communistic, I could not afford to even acknowledge such ravings until he sent me an affidavit that he was not now nor ever had been a member of the Party. I told him that I would not make a direct accusation, for perhaps he was only ignorant, but he had aroused my suspicion. To date, there has been no reply.

Let us go on the offensive. Rather than defend the National Council or the churches, let us carry the attack to these malicious and evil trouble-makers. All together now, boys, with one voice, let us proclaim the real issue! Whatever builds the Church and encourages true Christianity is raising a mighty fortress against communism. Whoever seeks to weaken the Christian witness is consciously or unconsciously following the Communist line.

## 32: Wives

An intellectual is a fellow who thinks there is something more interesting to talk about than women. Let it be confessed sadly, this old preacher is no intellectual and so a friend had little trouble recently in bringing the conversation around to the distaff side. However, we talked about a special kind of women, namely, preachers' wives.

Seems this friend is an executive big shot who has to deal with the problems of about five hundred pastors. He had been trying to prevent a divorce and had failed. He was feeling mightly low. According to his experience, this sort of thing does go on, and it seems to be increasing. The cause? "Well," said my friend, "too many wives are going to psychologists." This was so heretical that it shocked my conservative nature and I felt that such subversive doctrine should be challenged. "Explain!" I commanded, and this is what the man said.

The ministry is a tough job, and it puts more strain on preachers and their families than most professions. Today if anybody is not positively happy, he or she runs to a psychologist or a psychiatrist, or some kind of professional counselor. These brethren are usually well-meaning, and they are up to their ears in theories about personality frustrations and fulfillments. The only trouble is, my friend claims, they do not know any more about the ministry than a rabbit.

So they tell the wife that she needs to fulfill her own personality and be a person in her own right. They always conclude, my friend says, that the strain is caused by the wife being submerged by her husband's status. He gets all the notice and he holds all the prominent places. The gals feel that they are only "preachers' wives" and but shadows of reality. I tell you, it makes your heart bleed.

Now what is the solution? Why, the wives must have a career of their own. They must get somebody to look after the kids and start teaching school. Or they must get a job in a bookstore or take up interior decorating. One wife (so help me, this is what he told me) was advised to take up smoking to release her tensions. The trouble is that a preacher's wife has a certain position in the church to maintain. When she withdraws from the ministry, she ruins her husband.

Well, there my have been a time when churches were unreasonable in their demands on ministerial wives. But today few churches object to a woman being herself. She is no longer thought of as an unpaid member of the staff. She is seldom asked to do every chore no one else will do. She is a person and the ministry is a family affair. One of the main strengths of Protestantism is the family in the parsonage.

At this stage of the discussion, my friend became bitter. He said that there are too many of the psychological brethren who act as if persons can live in isolation. He said there are too many experts who think people can be healed apart from their social relationships. He said it was about time we recognize that if these counselors can do much good, they can also do much harm.

I have been pondering this and have arrived at four conclusions which are announced with great humility. *First,* to be a preacher's wife is a career without peer. *Second,* if a girl wants a separate career of her own, she ought not to marry a preacher. *Third,* every preacher and most laymen know that a man's ministry is shaped for good or ill by his wife. *Finally,* if the time comes when a preacher and his wife need help in their relationships, let them consult one who not only knows something about the human heart, but also something about the Protestant Church.

## 33: *Confession*

Every time there is a particularly notorious crime, some poor fellow gets an irresistible impulse to confess. At least that is the impression of a whodunit buff whose reading in the field is not inconsiderable. This is one of the stranger quirks in human nature, which is full of strange quirks. Is it a desire for publicity? Is it a desire to relieve the pressure of general guilt? Is it an expression of a deep-seated tendency toward lawlessness? Or is it just an escape from boredom? In any case, while confession done decently and in order is important, it is one of those things that can so easily go wrong.

The devout Catholic must find great release when he unburdens himself in the privacy of the confessional. Here is an opportunity to unload in a private and impersonal manner. The Protestant does not find it so easy unless he has learned to make his confession to God Himself. His pastor ought to be wise enough to preserve the reticent individual from painful embarrassment. If he turns to the group, he may get caught in the old Oxford house party which often became a kind of spiritual strip tease. I got caught in just one, and that ended that.

Now we have another problem: the desire on the part of some Protestatnt ministers to confess, with the unhappy results of too much in the wrong place at the wrong time. The idea is to organize a group, see? Meet together and talk about your problems until all the little ones have become big ones. Then, when you cannot stand it any longer, tell each other all the bad thoughts you have had and all the bad things you have done. Do not hold back anything, so that after a few meetings everybody knows everything about everybody. Get it? This is supposed to set you free, althought it resembles undressing in public.

Then, one day, one of these fine fellows gets angry with you and throws out a hint that what he knows about you is not so good. Or you get self-conscious when you remember what you said in an open meeting, and the relationships get a little strained. Or some nut decides to make what he hears the basis of a thesis or a book and quotes statistics on the sickness of the ministry. The statistics are based on something less than one millionth of one percent, but the generalities make a dandy chart. Then the meetings become a kind of magnet which draws every weak sister in the brotherhood, so that the participants resemble more and more a ward in a mental institution rather than a ministerial fellowship. And the boys who pontificate about the good that comes out of it are the sickest of the bunch.

Does a preacher need to confess? Yes, but let him find a friend he can trust and not be so naïve as to think that anything is secret when two other people know it. Let him explore the resources of his Christian faith and maybe take a little time to read his Bible. Let him know that in the world we all have tribulation, but there is One who has overcome the world. And let him test the promise of power to live by and discover the source of joy in his work. Unless the New Testament is false, men may walk with Christ and converse as friend with friend.

But this is all old-fashioned stuff and we crave the new psychological approach. Put it into that jargon if you prefer, but let us stay with the tested experience of men who have found that they who wait upon the Lord shall have their strength renewed. And let us have some sense of obligation to our ministerial profession. This constant whining about our troubles is giving the layman a cheap idea of the kind of men we are and the nature of the task we are called to perform.

## 34: *Termites*

The other day I saw a treasurer's report given to the monthly meeting of the official board of a small church. One item intrigued me mightily, and I wish there was some way to get more information about it. Here it is in all its splendid simplicity: *Payment for Termite Treatment—$12.50.* Doesn't that do something to you? Isn't it fine? Don't you wish you had someone to give that treatment to your church from time to time? For what brother among us does not have termites in his congregation, in his Sunday school, or maybe in the woman's society?

There was a fellow in one of my congregations who never could forget the depression and the big debts the church owed through most of the thirties. Every time we were ready to adopt a program that would make us stretch our financial muscles just a bit, he would get to his feet and launch into his speech. In lugubrious tones and with a bloodhound expression, he would tell of the terrible days when the bank threatened to foreclose every Monday morning. He bored on into the confidence of the people until they wept with self-pity and cried out for the fleshpots of slavery. Somebody would make a motion to defer, and the brave new vision would fade like the beautiful girl in the toothpaste advertisement who neglected her breath. I am in the market for a treatment for that termite.

There are churches being weakened by gossipers who pick up a lot of stuff that is not remotely related to facts. They drill into every conversation with some new scandal about the preacher or his family. The parsonage daughter was seen at a party wearing lipstick. The parsonage son was heard to use a bad word. If that mine runs out they try the choir director or the organist. They were seen in the church together five minutes before choir rehearsal on Thursday night. Indeed, anyone in any place of Christian responsibility will find these termites trying to chew up reputations. I saw an old church in Poland with an iron ring fastened to a chain and bolted to the wall near the door. Anybody guilty of slander had the ring locked around his neck, and the worshipers were encouraged to spit on him as they entered the church. I would prefer a less obvious treatment for termites, but those old boys had the right idea.

Or consider the church member who always says no. It does not make any difference what the proposition is or what the question asked. The response is always no. Offer him a thousand dollars and he will say no without thinking. Not a single thing has been accomplished in this termite's church during the twenty years he has been a member that has not been over his protest and in spite of his opposition. He has discouraged the youth and worn the preacher's nerves raw. If he can get enough to join him, he rots out the foundations of any godly plan.

Is there any treatment for these termites, and can we ever hope to dispose of them finally? Probably not, for even our Lord had one of them among his disciples. But in the church as in the battle the best defense is a strong offense. It is when the church has bogged down that the termites have opportunity to do their dirty work. Keep it marching and the people cannot hear their voices, nor can they feel their attacks. Subversion is only possible when people lose their way and stop traveling. The sound of a trumpet is one of the best termite treatments I know. On your feet, men, strike your tents and let's go!

## 35: *Panels*

The gripe—I mean the subject—for today, is panel discussions. I am afraid it is too late to do anything about this method of wasting time, for it has become firmly established in our mores. You just cannot have a conference or a program without some member of the committee bleating forth: "I think it would be nice to have a panel." The only sensible answer to the suggestion is "Why?" But to question this lowest form of communication is to label oneself as hopelessly out of step with the times. So we go along and we have a panel discussion.

We place between three and seven well-meaning citizens around a table on the platform, and we appoint a chairman—I mean a moderator. Now, the moderator is not supposed to do much talking except right at the beginning. He is to set the stage, so to speak, for the others. He introduces the members, and he must give the impression that each is an expert in his own field. He does the best he can with what he has to work with, and we are off.

There are always the same fellows on every panel. They have different names and they look different, but they are actually the same ones disguised. One is bashful and will only mumble a few words if he is put on the spot. He is probably the brightest one of the bunch, but he does not express himself well. His stammering is painful, and one wishes that he had written out a speech and read it. Another is the blunt type. He blares forth his opinion with assurance and with an air of "there will be no nonsense or even courtesy about this." The trouble is, he is not very bright.

There is always the fellow who explains what the other members of the panel really meant. Brethren, there is nothing more agonizing than to have this self-appointed interpreter explain you. He is the great leveler who makes every point of view grey and undistinguished. Then there has to be one cute guy. Sometimes it is a woman who hovers just on the edge of baby talk.

Every panel has a member who wants to dominate the show. He takes a long time to say very little, but he gets what he thinks is a new idea every time another member speaks. The chairman tries to ignore him, but he will utter his triteness unless the chairman tells him to kindly shut up. This, of course, is a little embarrassing.

But the worst thing about the whole process is the assumption that any subject can be treated profitably by a panel. I heard one on atomic power by people who knew no more about it than I do. Seven times zero is still zero. A few friends sitting around sharing their ideas, asking questions, expressing opinions, is one thing. Putting it in an auditorium is something else. I must confess that the law of averages works, and every now and then there will be a pretty good result. But there will be twenty fiascoes for the one success.

I overheard a Sunday school teacher talking about the Trinity. She finally summed it all up by saying, "It's a kind of heavenly panel." And I crept away in despair. I am not easily discouraged, and if I may say so, I am on the optimistic side quite often. But this remark has so broken my spirit that I have not smiled for days. The universe presided over by a panel is more horrible to contemplate than any hell imaginable.

Are there any men left who will stand and be counted? Dare we insist that if there must be a program, we will have a man stand on his feet and declare himself? We are homesick for a prophet with a "Thus said the Lord." Enough of these little wishy-washy conversations. Give us a speech. Make a pronouncement! I cannot believe that I alone am left of those who have not yet bowed the knee to this Baal. Preachers of the Word, arise!

## 36. *Sheep*

One of the wonderful titles given to the Christian minister is "pastor." It means, of course, a shepherd, and it had more meaning for a rural society than it holds for our industrial economy. But it still fills my heart with joy to hear a fine layman speak with loving appreciation of his pastor. Here is a unique relationship which we understand because we are the inheritors of the Bible and the hymnal.

It came to me the other day that the shepherd can fulfill his role properly only if he knows what it is to be a sheep. Maybe it ought to be said that the shepherd needs to realize that he, too, is a sheep. Ezekiel could be the comforter and guide of the exiles after—as he put it—" . . . I came to the exiles at Telabib, who dwelt by the river Chebar. And I sat there overwhelmed among them seven days" (Ezek. 3:15). The pastor, I take it, is the man who can enter sympathetically into the situation of the flock. So our Lord puts much emphasis on sympathy in the Beatitudes.

A shepherd might easily fall into the trap of considering the sheep only as a source of wool; or to put it in wordly parlance, they exist to be clipped. A man may give this attitude all kinds of high-sounding rationalisms, as: the good of the church, or the sheep's own good. After all, too much wool is neither healthy nor comfortable. But deep down, such a shepherd has no real concern for the sheep except as a source of support. Since a pastor is himself too often a victim of exploitation, he ought to know how the people feel about it.

If a minister has achieved a relatively comfortable status, he may forget what it is to be out of a job, or living on an economic level where an extra ten dollars is a serious problem. We are the shepherds of such sheep, and while we feel sorry for ouselves that we are not paid enough, there are those much worse off. Our middle-class Protestant churches create an illusion that no one is hurting financially. Don't you believe it!

The sheep of our pastures sometimes get the idea that church conferences pass resolutions recklessly. That is, they feel that this social justice we preach about is going to cost them money. The reforms we advocate mean sacrifice on somebody's part, and they suspect they are the chosen victims. They have a point. The man living in a house which costs him nothing for taxes or upkeep can be much less conservative when it comes to voting school bonds. This is not to advocate that we mute our prophetic voices, but that we have more sympathy for the ones who will pay a bigger price than we pay.

Most of all, however, we need to take personally the words of the 119th Psalm: "I have gone astray like a lost sheep" (v. 176). Let us join lustily and sincerely in the General Confession: "Almighty and most merciful Father; We have erred and strayed from Thy ways like lost sheep." The Twenty-third Psalm was written for preachers as well as laymen: "The Lord is *my* Shepherd . . ." (emphasis supplied). I doubt that the Shepherd has any more trouble with any of his sheep than he has with ministers.

No one today is flattered when he is referred to as a sheep. But just When I am ready to claim the status of being superior to the flock, I remember my own helplessness, my stubbornness, my stupidity. Then I recall that our Lord was called the Lamb of God and there is no record of his objection. Maybe the first thing we ought to do at the next meeting of the Ministerial Association is to say together:

> *For he is our God,*
> *and we are the people of his pasture,*
> *and the sheep of his hand.*
>
> Psalm 95:7

# 37: *Abstraction*

My text today is taken from a fellow named Joubert who was a very prominent French literary critic and moralist at the time of the French Revolution. He said on one occasion: "How many people become abstract as a way of appearing profound." Amen!

Who is most guilty of this sin? Philosophers? Perhaps. Most of them would rather be caught dead than be popular. Their heavy volumes with their deadly subjects are enough to frighten a man to death. But if such a man can overcome his fright and calmly analyze what is being said in the first chapter, he may discover it is quite ordinary stuff—even obvious. But put into the specialized lingo of philosophy, it sounds like the proclamation of a god who never knew a human emotion or experienced a divine ecstasy.

Maybe the theologian ought to have first place in this indictment. A good many of the scholars writing in this field are either first or close seconds. They are the cloister-boys who spin their scholastic theories and treat a tiny point as if it were the Washington Monument. Stripped of the high-flown verbiage, the whole thing becomes a nice little homily with no great depth and mighty little importance.

But now we come to a third nomination for this dubious award: preachers! And this, brethren, is terribly serious. For the philosophers and the theologians do amazingly little harm, but preachers who wallow in abstractions turn the greatest story ever told into a long and boring yarn. They make truth a lumbering agony and they make the Gospel dull as dishwater. That the Church has thus far survived abstract preaching is nothing less than a miracle.

The abstraction specialists talk only to each other. The congregation is never their first object of interest, and the men who prefer erudition to communication pride themselves that, if no one listens, this proves they are profound homileticians. Their sermons sound like the next chapter in a colorless book. I suppose that one of the decisions a man has to make is whether he will be an evangelist or an intellectual.

Let no man assume that there is a gap between the mind and the spirit. He is not to popularize at the cost of intellectual integrity. But neither is he to use abstractions as a cover-up for his own spiritual poverty. Without much personal experience of God, we can generalize until the cows come home. We begin to get embarrassed when a man in trouble, a woman at the breaking point, or a child asks us specifically what we can say about God. Then we long for the security of a pulpit and a well-mannered congregation who will listen politely to our pontificating. As the exiles longed for Jerusalem, we long for this safety.

To be concrete demands first-hand knowledge. It is always much easier to be abstract, so we sit back and criticize the men who speak to the people's needs and win a large following. You ought to listen to the boys in the back room tear apart any preacher whom the people hear gladly. It would be better to ask why they do not hear us gladly. Maybe it is because people are concerned with such problems as making the next payment on the car more than they are in listening to a discussion of the latest theological obscurity.

Brethren, may the good Lord deliver us from any ambition to be considered profound. May He fill us with a desire to tell the old, old story with grace and directness. May we know something about what God can do for others, because He has done so much for us. And when we see a life saved, it may come to us that this is pretty profound preaching after all.

# 38. *Elucidation*

One of the coaches of the San Francisco Giants was discussing baseball from the standpoint of the fans. "It's like church," he said. "Many attend but few understand." Wisdom comes from such unexpected sources, and that is why a preacher ought to be listening to any man who wants to speak to him. He may not get a new clue to the authorship of Hebrews, but every now and again he will hear a good word about life.

Now if you conduct your service in Latin, you are not concerned primarily with people understanding. Let them immerse themselves in mystery, and if the priest has a fair idea of what is going on, that is good enough. There is a point here certainly, for the priest, whether he is Protestant or Catholic, will only make a fool of himself if he thinks he can explain all of God's ways with His world. A good healthy dose of awe is necessary for every religious worshiper.

But we believe that Christianity is enlightenment as well as mystery. People go to church for guidance and inspiration, which they receive all too seldom. Religion comes to symbolize in their minds what is vague, obtuse, impractical. The hymns are so seldom sung as if the congregation were confessing its faith and expressing its hope. Does anyone look at the words and seriously consider what they mean? I heard a minister say in one service: "We shall sing hymn number 382, which sums up our belief about God's providence." I thought that was helpful.

I know one minister who has Bibles in the pews, and the congregation reads the Scripture lesson together. It is more effective than you might think, for it makes a man consider what the Book says when he has to put forth some effort to read it. Most of our psalters can stand improvement, and the so-called responsive reading can be detached and lifeless. We read, but we are not responsive, for the format and the way it is done does not encourage curiosity.

But worst of all and least excusable is the sermon's lack of clarity. Preachers would be shocked if they knew how little their people understand what they glibly rattle off on Sunday morning. We simply cannot purge our vocabularies of the theological terms which our laymen cannot even spell. We merely refer to matters of our conference or synod which we discuss every time we meet another minister. But our laymen have never heard about these doings, for many of us, dear brothers, act as if the less a layman knows about his church, the better. The loyal churchman is often like the fellow attacked for denying the Monroe Doctrine. "It's not true!" he shouted. "I love the Monroe Doctrine, I would die for the Monroe Doctrine! I only said I don't know what it is."

When we come to a day where hysterical reactionaries begin to attack church leaders, the great Christian social affirmations, or the National Council of Churches, we are horrified that good men are led astray so easily. We should blame ourselves. Always there will be a few who want their church to be a museum, but most members only need to be made aware of the social and ecumenical implications of the Gospel. I am not going to worry about how little baseball fans understand the game. But if church members do not understand their church, that is pretty serious. Elucidate, brethren, elucidate!

# 39: *Individuality*

I take my text today from a great journalist, Herbert Bayard Swope. He was talking primarily to newspapermen, but his words have relevance for another profession that uses words and deals with people. He said that, while the formula for success is hard to come by, the sure formula for failure is to try to please everybody. I hear some fellows say, "Wait a minute! How else does a minister get along, and how else can he stay in the same church more than a year?" Patience, brother, and I will tell you.

I have known a few preachers who spent all their time trying to please every family in the congregation. This really takes some doing, for these families range all the way from what appear to be leftovers from a prehuman species to the way-out folks from the world of tomorrow. Some want a fundamentalist and some want a crusader. This woman likes high-church services and this man wants the atmosphere of a country dance. Here is a family who want a real, folksy pastor, and over there is a family who want the sermon to sound like the rough draft of a Ph.D. thesis in philosophy. The point being that nobody can please all the members all the time, even in a fairly small congregation.

But as I was saying—I have known a few who tried. They made life unbearable for their children by keeping them home from the social functions at the school because old Mrs. Gloom disapproved. They forbade their wives to use a little make-up because sister Sour declared it was not scriptural. They made Sunday a good introductory experience for hell, so that no one could criticize the way the pastor and his family observed the Sabbath. But it was no good. The preacher and his family still got criticized, and they still had pressure to move after shorter and shorter pastorates.

A congregation and especially an official board soon sense when a preacher is scared. And even when power over another gives people some sinful satisfaction, they despise the fellow who is scared. The man who has a brave conviction receives the reluctant admiration of the critics. People resent the trimming of the message to suit their prejudices, even while they are screaming their loudest that if this is not done they will quit. The preacher who has nothing else to commend him but a puppy-like desire to be everybody's pal always comes to a bad end. If your enemy will not love you, make sure that he has to respect you.

Of course a man has to have a sense of propriety and not do the rude, crude things that antagonize unnecessarily. The fellow who has no concern for differing opinions and no respect for the dignity of every man will not have a happy time, and probably should never have entered the ministry in the first place. So what does it all add up to?

The congregation wants to respect a man for his sincerity, his honesty, his integrity. They want to believe that their pastor loves them even when he must oppose them. They are at ease if the preacher is associated with them on every level of their life. They want to feel sure that the man in the pulpit is not sounding off without a proper understanding of all that is involved. They would like to know that their pastor knows them and their testings, and that he sits where they sit. Then they forgive him when he does not always please them, for they prefer a man to a chameleon.

# 40: *Referral*

I was thinking the other day about how far the Church has moved toward becoming a mere referral agency. We become more and more like an information booth with someone saying to the people, "We don't have anything for you, but we can tell you where to get it."

Suppose a fellow comes to the church because he is hungry. What does the preacher say to him? He says, "Buddy, here is a ticket to the Salvation Army. Go down there and they will feed you." A neglected community needs a hospital and comes to the Church for help. "Well," says the Church, "if the government will pay for it, we might consider managing it if we can be assured there will be no financial commitment and no financial loss." We may have started a social center down in the slums, but today we find we must close it. Why? The community chest has cut our budget. If you want that work to continue, then you must put pressure on the budget committee of the chest to restore the cut.

Now preachers have fallen into the same habit. They no longer regard themselves as earnest, dedicated, trained men engaged in the cure of souls. They are counselors who have had a year at a mental institution—not as patients but as interns—and now they have office hours, and you have to get an appointment. Sometimes they will see as many as two or three people in one day. These people who come to them are not regarded as sheep without a shepherd or as members of the pastor's flock. No, sir, they are clients. So help me, that is what the boys are calling them now: CLIENTS! And one of the things they are warned about is not to treat people who are too sick. These must be referred—get it?—to some professional, often secular psychologist.

There was a time when the Church ministered directly to the people. The Church built the hospitals and the first movement toward feeding the hungry and caring for the poor and disinherited was instigated by the Church. The great medieval universities were created by the Church, which became the mother of education. Here is where men went seeking refuge and help. No longer. Now we have become selective and withdrawn from this business of giving men what they need.

Do you remember that incident in the story of the feeding of the five thousand recorded by Mark? The crowds followed Jesus around the lake, and instead of solitude he found the people waiting. He taught them, for he could never resist the needs of men, and the hour grew late. The disciples told him that he must send the people away to the villages where they could buy bread. But what was his response? He said: "You give them something to eat." They told him it was impossible, for they could not afford to buy enough bread to feed that crowd. But with his touch on them they did feed the multitude, and the story says there were bread and fish left over.

I have an uneasy feeling that Jesus may be saying the same thing to the modern Church. "You give them something. You be more than a referral agency." For I believe with all my heart that only the Church has what the world needs if it is going to be saved. Brethren, how about more feeding and less referring?

# 41 : *Modesty*

A fellow said he had a great shock the other day. He had assumed that some words were never to be spoken in the presence of ladies, and he had been careful that his wife should never hear them, at least from him. He had assumed that everybody felt this way, and that women never heard some of the expressions unfortunately familiar to the rougher sex. Then he happened to glance through a best seller his wife was reading and found six of the forbidden words in the first chapter. He was surprised and disillusioned.

It is amazing to note how naïve we are about keeping what we know from other people. You remember the old lady who heard of Darwin's theory of evolution and said, "God grant that it may not be true. But if it is true, God grant that not many people will hear about it." History seems to suggest that those who think knowledge can be confined to certain classes are not very realistic. Ideas have a habit of getting around.

Preachers have been guilty of this attempt to keep certain things to themselves rather than stir up the people. We have raised a generation of milk-fed church members because nobody ever gave them any meat. Maybe a young seminary graduate got into trouble for preaching the documentary theory of the Pentateuch and resolved never to mention anything that might upset his people again. Or some old watchdog of orthodoxy sat on the front row every Sunday morning and tried to spot a slight tendency toward theological heresy. The preacher decided to say nothing rather than take a chance.

Well, let us confess that neither the higher nor the lower criticism as ends in themselves, makes for helpful or inspiring preaching. Let us recognize that preaching one's doubts will not grow Christians or build the Church. But let us realize also that our churches are full of intelligent people who would like to know more about the Bible than they learned in their primary Sunday school class. They would be interested in hearing something about Christian theology which would take them a step or two farther than the junior curriculum. We would be surprised by the number of church members who could be interested in church history and the story of their own denominational tradition.

Now and then, we may bruise a tender blossom who prefers to be Peter Pan rather than a soldier of the Cross. But we have no right to keep the soldiers unarmed in order to protect the blossom. Certainly the majority of Christians want to grow, and we sin against them and the future when we keep everything we learned at seminary a deep, dark secret. Let every minister get over the idea that what the people do not know won't hurt them. It will hurt them and the Church very much. Let the people know about the wonder of the Bible revealed by the scholars, the critics, the archeologists, and the historians. Teach your members some of the theological mysteries revealed to great theologians.

Some small groups in a church that do more than wallow around in self-analysis would be a wonderful thing. The schools have decided that in a world like ours something more is necessary than enrichment courses to help children adjust. Maybe the time has come for the Church to regard its people not as babes but as men. It seems to me that it was a Protestant idea that the Book should be opened to the people. Now, if we can get over our fear of shocking them, we may be on the road to maturity.

# 42. *Compliments*

A few of the boys were sitting around one Sunday night in a rather relaxed mood. They were telling about the events of the day, trying to intimate subtly that their churches had been full and the sermons had been first-class. It was such a welcome relief from watching them drip self-pity that I rejoiced when one of them asked brazenly: "What was the most appreciated compliment you ever received on a sermon?" They sat back for a moment's reflection and then were off on a group therapy voyage that will be long remembered.

One fellow said his best compliment had come from his finance committee last year when they recommended a substantial increase in his salary. This was regarded as just a little on the flippant side, but we did agree that such a vote of confidence does lift up a man's spirit. Most preachers are not commercially minded, although most of them welcome some extra dollars to keep them on the economic level of the custodian, at least. But when a church votes to raise a salary, it is saying in very loud language: "We believe in you and we appreciate you." Would that the good Lord would inspire more laymen with a desire to say it with cash.

The next brother said his best response had come from an eight-year-old boy who had marched straight up to the preacher at the close of the sermon and said, "I liked that sermon." Seems that no one had put him up to it, and something in the sermon appealed to the youngster. It takes a kind of genius to preach to children. But if our words are plain and our delivery natural, they will often give such an honest response that a man feels more honored than by the accolades of a dozen adults. I knew how he felt, for children have not yet learned to lie or flatter and their simple thanks shine in that light.

Another preacher said that he remembered an old lady who was a saint. She said to him one day, "Pastor, you gave me a new vision of Jesus Christ." He said that it would not have meant much coming from some people, but here was one who was a mature Christian with a deep grasp of the riches of the Gospel. That he had been able to give her a new vision pleased him very much.

But the compliment that impressed me most was given by a teen-age girl who had said with a shining face, "Dr. Smith, it is so exciting to hear you preach." How do you like that one? How often is a man worthy of it? How many are ever worthy of it? Is this the accepted idea of a sermon? Oh, my dear friends, I have to confess that more often our sermons are synonyms of dullness, boredom, and monotony! To have a teen-ager say it is exciting to hear a man preach ought to send him up into the seventh heaven—or higher.

When Jesus talked, the common people heard him gladly. The crowds became so interested in his teaching that they forgot about food. They marveled at the way he put things, and they had never believed that religion could be so thrilling. The whole thing seemed suddenly relevant and central.

Well, let us try and get excited ourselves. Let us speak of persons and not of systems nor of humanity in general. Let us speak of the spiritual and the unseen as if they were real. Let us speak of freedom and hope. Let us see life in its drama and its high purpose. In a word, let us preach the Gospel.

Now I live with a great hope that one day a man or a woman, a boy or a girl, will say to me, "It is exciting to hear you preach." When that time comes, I will know that on at least one occasion I was not far from the Kingdom of God.

# 43. *Quitter*

I saw an article the other day in one of our secular magazines with the intriguing title "Why I Quit the Ministry." It was written anonymously by a young Presbyterian minister, who tells of his many disappointments with his people. It seems the laymen were not consecrated Christians, nor would they heed his admonitions and become real Christians. It was enough to make a man weep at all this poor young man had to endure. After all was said and done, he just could not take it any longer and he quit.

The situation he described is not a new one. A long time ago there was an associate pastor named Demas, who walked out because, according to St. Paul, he was "in love with this present world." But this modern fellow denies that this is his reason. He says the people refused to care, and he cannot justify devoting his life to an organization made of such ingrates. This high-sounding reason for quitting gets less respect from me than I feel for poor old Demas.

Who is this pure young knight who finds the sinners of the Christian church too low-down to serve? There is not a man in the ministry who has not encountered all the types he catalogues and worse. But along with them there are the quiet saints who shame the pretensions of the man in the pulpit. There are the responses, the awakenings, the joyful sacrifices made for Christ's sake. When any man lives with a congregation for three years and finds nothing there but disappointment, you can be sure—and this is putting it as charitably as possible—he was never called to the ministry. When he finds nothing in the fellowship of his ministerial brethren but competition and political maneuvering, he is sick, sick, sick.

Now since this noble lad has left the Church, to whom shall he go?

Well, he is going to study sociology and teach in a university. Fine. But when these inspired young people come out of his classes, where are they going to take their inspiration? To the DAR? the American Legion? the labor union? the service club? If he goes into public service, will the Democrats or the Republicans or the independents give him the support he craves? Pardon my smiling.

For this eloquent young quitter and all his ilk, George Bernard Shaw had a word. He told of a contemporary who had resigned his seat in Parliament rather than compromise his principles. And he thought back over his own smirched character, which had been blackened by struggling to make a little progress here and preventing a retreat there. "I do think," he wrote, "Joe might have put up with just a speck or two on those white robes of his for the sake of the millions of poor devils who cannot afford any character at all because they have no friends in Parliament. Oh, these moral dandies, these spiritual toffs! These superior persons! Who is Joe anyhow that he should not risk his soul occasionally like the rest of us?"

There was a man in the New Testament who was the archetype of these preachers who quit because the people are not worthy of them. He prayed thankfully that he was not as other men. As I recall, he was not held up as a hero.

# 44: *Choir Directors*

I would like to request that what is said here will not be passed on any further. If it should get back to my choir director or to my music committee, I will be looking for a job. So this is just between us.

I am fed up with certain qualities certain choir directors develop. I have been around long enough to know that it is better to let things alone in this department rather than complain or criticize. Hell hath no fury like musicians on the rampage. So most of us go along year after year with the status quo lest a worse fate befall us. If the fellow is a fair musician, we let him rule his kingdom even when every Sunday our sense of worship is outraged and we suspect that we are being robbed both financially and religiously.

For instance, why is it that these fellows cannot tell time? Why is it that they must practice until exactly eleven o'clock or one minute after? How many times a minister goes into his pulpit without calmness of spirit because he has had to herd the choir in on time. Added to that far from inspiring task, he has listened to a frantic director give last minute directions so that everybody is confused and nervous.

One time, just once, I knew I could stand it no longer. I called a meeting of the music committee after church and told them they could fire either the choir director or me. I did not much care which, but they were not going to have both of us around any longer. You will find it hard to believe this, but they fired the director.

What is the point of a divided chancel if the choir director has to place his music rack and a platform right in the center and stand in front of the altar? Then while he motions until everybody is standing where he wants him to stand, the congregation is transported out of the church into a concert hall. And most of them never get back into the church again that morning. Is the choir to put on a performance for an audience? It was a more honest arrangement when the choir sat behind the pulpit facing the congregation. While their whispering and gum-chewing now and then added little to the worship service, at least it was not necessary to move so much stuff when they performed. Is there a voice in the land that will suggest that choirs ought to be directed discreetly and unobtrusively? Is there much point in making the altar the center if it is to be obscured by some fellow waving his arms?

That leads me to another point. Can nothing be done with these directors, both men and women, who seem to be taking their setting up exercises as they direct? It always seems to me that they conceive music to be something that is produced by sheer physical effort. The trouble is that there is no relation between their strenuous efforts and the quality of the music they draw out. Quite the opposite. Usually, the more athletic they become, the less desirable is the quality of the anthem. Men will not be heard for their much speaking, and choir directors are not to be chosen for their much arm action.

The choir director who is only a musician and not a churchman ought to be directed elsewhere. For the church is God's house and the place where we come to be met and to meet Him. I shall not forget the experience of hearing a boys' choir, out of sight, in a Spanish cathedral. But the fellows I am talking about come to be seen. Now and again one of them will even wave his arms when the congregation sings a hymn. Cheerleaders are all right, I guess, at a football game, although the whole affair seems a little silly to me now. But may the good Lord deliver us from their tribe in church.

# 45: *Rivers*

I read the other day about a poker game that has been going on for years. It is played every morning and every evening on a New York commuter train that runs along the Hudson River. One morning a man happened to glance up from the game and look out the window. "Look, fellows," he called out in surprise. "There's a river." I thought, there are some rivers we miss because we are involved in too many secondary affairs. They flow by us but we do not see them. You will remember, of course, the vision of St. John in the Revelation (22:1-2): "Then he showed me the river of the water of life, bright as crystal, flowing from the throne of God and of the Lamb through the middle of the street of the city . . ." Not many people see that one.

How often the Bible talks about springs, streams, rivers. One of its most persistent images is of weary men traveling through dry places and being led to the living waters. It is a good thing for the minister to remember that he is a shepherd leading his flock out of the waste-land into the green valleys where the springs are. Get that dry, arid stuff out of the sermon, brother, and replace it with something green and growing. The people have been parched all week and they come seeking refreshment.

But the preacher himself needs to find a river. He must preach Sunday, and the well has gone dry. There was not a sermon in the last issue of his favorite magazine that refreshed him. There was nothing in the morning paper to attack with any conviction. Nobody said anything inspirational at the Rotary meeting. The stuff on television ought not to be brought into a bar, let alone a church. What to do?

Try the Bible. It is like a spring of water welling up forever. You can hardly read a page without getting excited by a word, an insight, an idea. Believe me, preachers would be in a bad way indeed without this ever flowing river of truth and inspiration. It is a pity when men get so engrossed in the contemporary world that they forget this view of the eternal one.

Sometimes a preacher will get so overwhelmed with opposition that he thinks the whole congregation is against him. A few people can make much noise and a few loud voices can give the impression they speak for the majority. Nearly always there is a river of love flowing by the study if you will look up. Most of the people have not joined the enemy but, as has been their custom from the beginning, stand by their minister.

When the whole world seems to be going wrong, put it down partly to the fact that nearly all we see printed or hear broadcast is bad news. Read the testimony of a man like Frank Laubach and learn that "the world is learning compassion." There is a river of kindness flowing from nation to nation and around the world. Every missionary is part of that river and every Christian adds to its flow. Just when you decide that people are no good, then you see—if you are looking—some amazing kindness and a heart-warming expression of concern.

Brethren, there is a river of devotion flowing through your church. There are saints whose loyalty puts our own to shame. There are families who have made the church the center of their lives, and they give it first claim on their time. There are men whose testimony is always brave and clear. There are women who could rule society and have chosen to be the servants of Christ. May the good Lord deliver us from the blindness of those poker players who had a mighty river flowing outside their window and saw it not.

# 46: *Status Quo*

Sir Henry Bessemer, inventor of a new method for making steel, was asked to comment on his discovery. He said, "I had an immense advantage over many others dealing with the problem inasmuch as I had no fixed ideas derived from long-established practice to control and bias my mind, and did not suffer from the general belief that whatever is, is right." Being one of those homiletic scavengers always on the lookout for scraps overlooked by others, I picked this one up and then decided it might serve preachers better than laymen.

The curse of our calling, brethren, is professionalism. It makes us more desirous of protecting our status than saving souls. We would rather die in rigid respectability than risk being caught with our dignity down. This attitude is not usually deliberate or conscious but the result of spiritual paralysis and a hardening of the arteries of the imagination. It is a serious sickness and not easily healed.

One thing that will help us is to listen to young men just entering the ministry. Much of their stuff is impractical and impossible. But in the freshness of their vision we can often catch a glimpse of our pretenses and our dullness. Now and again one of these boys comes up with a fresh approach and a new way that will work. Give them a hearing, O wise Elders, and if it lieth in you, give them a chance to try it out.

A layman now and again spots a foolish procedure that we have looked at so long we no longer see it. True, many a layman speaks with limited knowledge, and his idea is not applicable to the Church. But the Christian fellowship which listens to laymen will be closer to relevance than the one that is priest-ridden. The attitude of the amateur can sometimes enlarge the vision of the professional.

The renewal of the Church comes usually from a man outside the hierarchy. It took the Prophet of Nazareth to see the sin of turning the Temple into a den of thieves. It was a relatively unknown monk who revealed the whole sordid business of selling indulgences to fill the pope's treasury. It was a priest of the Church of England not standing very high with the bishops who brought the warmth and power of Christianity back into eighteenth-century England. So it goes. None of these were bent on starting new churches, but the professionals, sometimes referred to as "the old war horses" took a dim view of these unimportant amateurs. And let me whisper something to you, men. All these renewers were persons who "did not suffer from the general belief that whatever is, is right."

The president of the Carnegie Foundation once remarked that the last act of a moribund corporation is to issue an enlarged edition of the rule book. Ah me! What was that last document that came down from headquarters? What is that instruction from the bishop's office or that advice from the board secretary? Courage! Even at this eleventh hour it may be that some plain Christian is getting ready to blow his trumpet and shatter the walls of the bogged-down institution. Then God, who delighteth in confounding the mighty, will start His children moving again. Amen!

# 47. *Parents*

I preached in a neighboring church the other Sunday and had a miserable time. My frustration finds no balm because there does not seem to be anything to do about it. The sanctuary was no cathedral, but it was quite satisfactory. It had a pulpit, an organ, a choir, and some pews. It had a congregation that filled the pews.

But there were present a family with a baby and another family with a restless child who talked. I saw it coming right from the beginning, but when the hymns are being sung, or the anthem is loud, a fellow tries to forget these threats. He even hopes that the baby will go to sleep and that the child is anxiously waiting to listen quietly to the sermon.

Well, the time came for me to preach. The sermon may have been no great shakes, but it was my best. I had worked on it all week, and here was the half hour for which all the hours of labor had been given. This, as the fellow said, was the big moment.

I got started pretty well, and the congregation was awake and responsive. Then the baby let out a howl somewhere in between joy and anguish. The mother and father beamed appreciatively as if to say that nothing so important had ever taken place in that church. Mrs. Kennedy says I paused and glared, but she has a tendency to exaggerate in such situations. I went bravely on.

Soon the small child dropped a book and asked in a loud voice if he could get a drink. He was shushed properly. The baby now came to life again and gurgled and cooed, again to the obvious pride of the parents. Along toward the conclusion of the sermon, which by this time was a complete ruin, the baby got the hiccups. Brethren, have you ever tried to conclude between hics?

But there was more to come. At the conclusion of the service, the father and mother laughingly related how their baby could not be kept quiet, and the other couple told me that they believe in bringing their child to church "right from the beginning."

Even to have reported this may seriously jeopardize my future. Preachers are supposed to put up with anything, and to say a critical word about children in the service is worse than being accused of subversion. Who dares to tell these insensitive parents that they are killing a preacher and upsetting a congregation? Who has courage to proclaim that the worship service is not the place for noisy, restless youngsters?

Now let me be clear. I believe the church ought to be family-centered. I believe that children should have the experience of worship. I believe that a church ought to furnish a nursery. But I do not believe that parents have any right to bring their children to the worship service when they cannot be quiet. When our Lord said, "Let the little children come unto me," he was not standing in a pulpit and he was not preaching a sermon. There is a time and place for all things.

One Sunday night when two little girls were running up and down the aisle, I asked the preacher whose they were. He said, "Mine," and I was so discouraged I never got the sermon off the ground. Once in a seminary chapel a noisy baby ruined me, and it turned out to be the offspring of a student preacher. Such men are not preachers and ought never to be allowed in a pulpit. It is bad enough to suffer the results of sin without actually encouraging it.

Finally, three suggestions. First, let some board secretary prepare an anonymous tract on this subject which the preacher can have circulated. He could do something with "if meat make my brother to offend," and so forth. Second, let the seminary counseling departments develop a technique to be used on parents who either cannot read or do not understand that any suggestion is to be taken personally. Third, let us raise a defense fund for the preacher who may get caught in the cross fire between parents and the group discussion boys. Thus endeth the lesson!

# 48: *Nightmare*

A man's dreams are not very interesting to another man unless he is a psychiatrist. The fellow who corners you and then proceeds to tell you of a long and involved dream is not my idea of a brilliant conversationalist. Dreams reveal a good deal about a man's subconscious, for all I know. Freud and Havelock Ellis held forth at some length on the sexual significance of these sleep adventures, but I still say that usually they are dull. Now let me tell you about a dream I had the other night.

I dreamed that all the Protestant churches in the United States became one organic union. Everybody rejoiced, and there seemed to be a general assumption that our chief problem had been solved. Nobody beat his breast on Wednesday for the sin of our divisions and then insisted on Sunday that only certain Christians could be allowed at the Lord's Table. Not a single prophet thundered his denunciations against our differences on Thursday and then proclaimed a narrow creed on Sunday. No one questioned another denomination's ministry or argued about who or what constitutes the true Church. Peace! It was wonderful.

Then the dream changed and a cold wind began to blow. This big institution had twenty times as much machinery as any minister had been caught in before. That meant, of course, thirty times as many committee meetings. The boards increased at an alarming rate, and all of them began to flood the preachers with their literature. Mailmen with more than one church on their routes went on strike. Church secretaries were not employed on the basis of their personalities and skills but according to their ability to lug tons of mimeographed stuff about the office.

Protestants with their traditional distrust of authority sought to conduct the business through traditional methods. There were conferences, assemblies, workshops, institutes. The trouble was that everybody spent so much time not offending others and making sure they were not being offended by others that nothing could be done. Some of the optimistic brethren who had been preaching this union for years sweetly counseled patience and said this was a temporary price well worth paying for union. In the meantime, nothing was accomplished.

But the main difficulty was an increasing tension which became more apparent with every passing month. The low-church boys were put out with the high-church fellows. The liturgical experts made some snide remarks about the Quaker-inclined worshipers. While this had been a problem before union, with only one church there was no place to go. It was like a family that had enjoyed one another on Christmas but was now forced to live all year in one house. Traits which had appeared just a little eccentric and interesting now became downright irritating.

Then a strange thing was observed. The stimulation of godly competition was gone, and nobody cared much about keeping alert to the need for extension and growth. Somehow it seemed less important. The vitality of the Baptists no longer troubled the Methodists. The witness of the Presbyterians was not now a challenge to the Episcopalians. Everybody was at ease, and the church consoled itself with vague references to quality instead of quantity, as if the two were antithetical. And then there was talk about a revolution brewing and the threat of a splinter group considering going its own way again.

It was at this point that Mrs. Kennedy poked me awake and said, "What kind of a nightmare were you having? You were groaning as if you were in mortal anguish." I smiled happily and mumbled: "I was, my dear. Thank you for waking me up."

# 49: *Intentions*

Many years ago, I played golf once a week with a good friend who was one of the world's worst preachers. Everybody knew it but him, and although he had other gifts, it was agony for the congregation to endure his sermons. Yet I never asked him how it had gone on Sunday that he did not tell me, "Fine." And then, before I could switch the conversation, he would give me the outline of his sermon and tell me how well it had been received. He would emphasize how outspoken he had been and how he had surely laid it on the line. Like a fool, I always let myself in for this rehash by not having courage to say firmly that enough was enough.

I have thought about that fellow off and on for many years. He stands as an example of all us poor preachers who do not know how bad we are. The only ones who seem to have any doubts are the good ones; the bad ones are sure they are great. I got a clue to the reason for this the other day in something John Ciardi wrote in the *Saturday Review*. He was talking about bad writing, and he said the bad writer sees only what he intended to write and what he was moved to write. "He never sees what he has actually written." Suddenly I saw the light. Poor preachers never hear what they have actually preached, but only what they intended, and unfortunately there is a world of difference.

We need to ask for grace to believe that other people's reaction to the sermon is better criticism than our own impression. One of the best sermons I ever preached was received with less than enthusiasm by my wife. I knew she was wrong, but with the passing years I have come to the conclusion that, wrong or right, her reaction is more likely to represent the congregation's than my own. Somewhere there

97

is an honest man or woman who will tell us if we ask for it. While this is one of the most painful experiences, we had better endure the pain and get some idea of what we really said and not what we intended to say.

The old professor who drones away over his lecture without any concern for the students' reactions will get by if he has tenure. But the preacher had better pay some attention to the reaction of the congregation. If they are being reached they will show it, and—believe it or not—general boredom is not the inevitable attitude of people in church. At any rate, the congregation makes the decision, and whether we agree with it or not we had better heed it. For when they signal thumbs down, the preacher has received the death sentence.

I suppose the truth is that, in anything like preaching, we must distrust our own judgments and lean heavily on others. The novelist who cannot get a publisher so often assumes that his book is too brave, too good, too original to be accepted by unimaginative editors. Don't you believe it, men. It is just too unsalable. So for the preacher who goes on believing that his stuff is too spiritual or too wonderful for run-of-the-mill congregations. They are right and you are wrong, brother, and until you come to terms with this fact there is no hope for you. All hail the man who at least intends to be a good preacher— but several times all hail the man who knows there is a big gap between the intention and the actual production!

So I go back to my old friend and his dream world. I suspect he lived a happier and perhaps an easier life by staying in it. But he would have been a better preacher if he had not confused intention with accomplishment. And so would we all.

# 50: *Controversy*

I was present at a meeting the other day when a prominent preacher was introduced to speak on a controversial subject. This in itself ought to make the headlines, since many of our preachers would rather be caught stealing than facing any vital issue. The fellow who gave the introduction said that this preacher was sometimes regarded as a controversial figure, but he was regarded universally as a man of integrity and courage. Then I began to raise some questions within myself about the whole subject of controversy.

The first question was, what kind of questions could a man deal with which are not controversial? How many things can a person talk about without risking the possibility of a difference of opinion? And if there is a difference of opinion, the result is controversy. We might discuss the weather, but even there we find some like it hot and some like it cold. How about heaven? The nice thing about that subject is that nobody can prove much. I read a book a few years ago written by a man who claimed he had been there and returned, but such experts are mighty few. Still, there are many people with rather strong ideas about the subject, and they differ with each other. It used to be safe to talk about Mother, but in our day we blame what is wrong with us on our parents. So you might run into trouble on that trail.

Since nearly everything has a controversial tinge to it, maybe the best thing to do is become an "on the one hand, and on the other" kind of preacher. You know the type. He was described by a listener who said he was not quite sure what the preacher was trying to say, but he seemed dedicated to the idea of not offending anyone. Even here, however, the results are not always salutary and safe. The fellow in the middle so often gets thrown at by both sides.

Then I asked myself another question. Is the Gospel noncontroversial? Jesus did not find it so; neither did Paul, Peter or the other Apostles. Of course they were all living in pagan environments, while we live in a country that has been officially Christianized. However, Martin Luther found a number of the brethren who did not see eye to eye with him, and John Wesley faced mobs that made him long for the safety of a den of lions. I looked around me at the contemporary leaders of the churches. Every one of them is under fire from one source or another and most of them have walked through dark valleys of opposition during most of their ministry.

So I came to a conclusion. To be a Christian means to be a controversial figure. To be a preacher means to be a warrior against the hosts of darkness that sometimes sneak into churches and get into city government. If any man ever refers to me as a noncontroversial figure, I shall demand an apology. May the good Lord deliver us from the namby-pamby, watered-down Christianity of our age and give us the courage to rejoice when our attack draws fire. And may we be able to do all this in love.

When a preacher reported to John Wesley on his travels about a circuit, he was asked if he had won any converts. He sadly confessed he had not. Had he made anyone angry? He brightened up and said no. Whereupon Wesley turned away in despair as if the man were hopeless. Our fathers thought that anger was often a sinner's first response. So does the Book of Acts. Where there is no controversy, the people perish.

# 51 : *Epitaphs*

I have been thinking about epitaphs, which indicates the state of my mind in these days. We do not go in for big stones as we once did, and epitaphs are not of so much personal and family concern as in years past. Still, there is something intriguing in considering a simple statement which might adequately sum up a man's line.

It is reported that W. C. Fields once suggested as his words of remembrance: "I would rather be here than in Philadelphia." While that sentiment expresses an opinion, it does not say much about the character of the man. There is a grave on Boot Hill in old Tombstone, Arizona, with just about the saddest words I have ever read. The old marker gives the name of George Johnson and the date of his death with this added note: "Hanged by mistake."

Somewhere in the Old West, this farewell report is placed over a grave:

> To LEM S. FRAME,
> who during his life shot 89 Indians,
> whom the Lord delivered into his hands,
> and who was looking forward to making up
> his hundred before the end of the year,
> when he fell asleep in Jesus
> at his house at Hawk's Ferry,
> March 27, 1843.

If this arouses your interest you will find many more in *Stories on Stone* by Charles L. Wallis (Oxford, 1954).

But we must not forget the fine epitaph which Thomas Jefferson wrote to be inscribed on his tomb. You will recall that he died on

July 4, 1826, the fiftieth anniversary of the Declaration of Independence. Out of the many things which he might have desired men to remember about him, he chose these:

> Here was buried
> THOMAS JEFFERSON,
> author of the Declaration of American Independence,
> of the statute of Virginia for religious freedom,
> and father of the University of Virginia.

Had he forgotten that he was President of the United States?

It would be interesting to learn what a man chooses out of his life as worth remembering. A lot of nice things are said about a fellow when he is making a speech away from home. But most of it is of dubious value, to say nothing about its accuracy. It is a flower presented kindly, and about as fragile. Not even the most egotistical could bear to see it carved in stone. What has a man done, what witness has he made, and what cause has he fought for that he wants recorded? This is a sobering thought to me and not at all comforting. Of one thing I am certain: that my epitaph would not take much space.

But God is merciful, and he lets us do a little good here and share a burden there, so that it does not have to be carved out on stone or spelled out in an obituary. Somebody says, "You helped me." A man remembers that you did not pass by on the other side of the street. A child recalls a real concern that made his resolutions stronger. All of this is written in the hearts of people and on their minds. Most of the stuff you can write down is not very important.

I started out talking about epitaphs, and here I am thinking about life. The great thing about the Gospel is that when you begin with the Cross, you end up with the Resurrection. You may start with burdens, but you come out with freedom. And if we do not always win, and our life ends in what seems to be defeat, we can say with the Irish patriot Robert Emmet: "Let there be no inscription upon my tomb. Let no man write my epitaph. I am here ready to die . . . Let my character and motives repose in obscurity and peace, till other times and other men can do them justice."

## 52: *Depth*

Have you ever noticed how quickly words and phrases wilt? What was fresh and crisp suddenly takes on the quality of day-old lettuce. We get hold of an expression which still has the dew on it, and before we know what has happened it has become stale, exaggerated, and unprofitable. What had truth in it becomes distorted and misleading. You will find it hard to believe, but my wife intimates from time to time that my vocabulary needs constant refreshing.

I was thinking about this the other day when for the tenth time somebody talked about something or other "in depth." The fellow was mentioning a survey, or a study, or a project, or a program—I forget which. But I do remember that it had to be "in depth." It always has to be in depth. Well, you may ask, what is wrong with doing things in depth? It is a good question, and since you have insisted, I will expound that matter for a moment.

Depth psychology seems to be pretty good stuff, but I read about a scholar in Vienna who thought we needed some height psychology. Seems that we can wallow around in the basement of our minds too long, so that our wills atrophy. What do you think of that? Maybe preachers are called to preach the good news of life's height possibilities as well as its depth and breadth.

I know some preachers who tackle every problem or discuss every subject as if they were digging a well. Brother, they can go down deep all right, but by the time they come to the surface, the congregation has directed its attention elsewhere. These fellows are very proud of their depth, and they would not be caught speaking plainly or interestingly for all the wedding fees in Reno. They have harsh words for the popular speakers whom the common folks hear gladly. But I must stop before I make a plea for shallower preaching.

Or take this matter of evangelism. There is emerging from our seminaries today a generation of young preachers who have been trained to be suspicious of sudden decisions, numbers, and goals. Why? Because men must be converted gradually and in depth. Quite so! But when a family decides to join a church and starts attending regularly, should we assume that nothing more is going to happen to them religiously? What is wrong with the church being a school of Christ for its members? The Presbyterians and the Methodists did this with the crowds who made decisions at the camp meetings more than a hundred years ago. The early Church did it with the revival results of Pentecost.

Let's face it: it is easier to work with a small group than to create an evangelistic fellowship which never lets a week pass without winning people to Christ and the Church. Enlisting laymen as visitation evangelists is hard work, and so is developing and maintaining a program. Keeping up with the population explosion demands sweat and weariness. Doing it in depth is sometimes another word for taking it easy.

There was an earthquake one night in a Philippian jail. The jailer was scared and wanted to know how to be saved. A Christian missionary named Paul said: "Believe in the Lord Jesus, and you will be saved, you and your household." Pretty shallow answer according to our depth boys. But only a beginning, as is every man's decision for Christ.

The next time a man says to me that we must wait until we take a depth survey before we act, I am going to say to him: "You wait. There are some folks in the next block who are not getting along very well. I am going to tell them about Christ in the simplest language I know. Maybe the Holy Spirit will take care of the depths."

# 53: *Institution*

Somebody said one time that no idea can outlive its institutionalization. It may have been George Bernard Shaw—at least it sounds like him. But whoever it was, the idea is sound, and it has particular relevance to the Christian Church, hence to preachers. When one compares the example and teaching of our Lord and then looks at the First Christian Church of Centerville, he will shudder if he has any sensitivity left. What has happened to the proclamation, the witness, the example? The institution has cerain admirable qualities, no doubt, but what ever happened to the Idea?

Yet institutions are inevitable, and no idea can long survive without organization. These pure spirits who find the Church too imperfect for their rarified natures, give me a pain. The sanctified soul that stays away from the Church because he might meet a hypocrite is of about as much account in the world as the perpetual student at the theological seminary who spends his years getting ready to do something he never starts. The answer, dear brethren, is not withdrawing into the smug superiority of some small society of gnostics. For the Church is not an option but an essential.

Here is the place where we have to deal with the paradox—that proposition so dear to the hearts of the modern theological eggheads. The idea cannot survive the institutionalizing and the idea cannot exist without the institutionalizing. How do you like that one? Or to put it in another way, which I picked up reading a book of theology I could not understand, the Church must wage a constant battle against itself.

Now the fellow who has to wage this battle is the minister, and he himself is the person it must be waged against first of all. The problem is how to take the office seriously and not to take the fellow who fills the office seriously. I must laugh at myself, but not at the ministry. I must be humble about my abilities and proud of my calling. I must believe that God has chosen me for the greatest task in the world, and I must cry out constantly for God's forgiveness of my egocentricity and inadequacy.

If we can succeed at all in this necessary task, we may then be fit instruments for the salvation of the Church. For the preacher is the one to keep the Idea ever before the people and make it shine through the endless activities and meetings. It is for him to keep the congregation aware of its responsibilities and duties. The voice in the pulpit is the voice of the prophet who thunders God's hatred of feasts and solemn assemblies. There is hope for the Church only as long as its ministry is sensitive to the essential enmity between an institution and a dream.

I wish I knew how to give advice in this field. But just when a glorious anger is hurled against the institution's denial of the spirit, the devil blunts the sharp edge of the preacher's witness at another point. This kind of evil comes out only with much prayer and fasting. All we can say for sure is that the ministry has no higher or more difficult demand than to be the instrument in God's hand to save the Church from itself. But that is not possible until we have allowed the grace of God to save us from ourselves. He is able if we are willing. Let us spend fifteen minutes every day examining ourselves and our Church in the light of the teaching and example of Jesus Christ.

## 54 · Best

That rare and admirable man, Don Marquis, married a woman who was a sincere and devoted Christian Scientist. Marquis, having no church of his own, although he had deep religious longings, agreed to become a part of his wife's religious group. He tried to live up to his decision, but it was no good. He just could not feel at home, nor did he find anything he was seeking. He claimed it was Mrs. Eddy's poetry which barred him, and he could never understand how such an extraordinary woman in many respects could have written such bad verse. And in any case, why did she publish it? Apparently none of the faithful were willing or able to keep it out of print. Marquis' one suggestion was that it should be translated into Hebrew or Greek, left as an obscure appendix for one hundred years, and then put back into English by a real poet.

Have you ever noticed the tendency of religious people to assume that if a thing is obviously religious, all its defects are to be excused? The music written by the church organist or choir director is to be admired, and worst of all, played, because the composer was a good Christian. The novel which has a good moral theme and encourages young people to believe that virtue is its own reward is to be read by all Christian parents and young people. That it is badly written has nothing to do with the case. Let the janitor's cousin paint a picture of Christ, and although it makes an artist so sick he turns green, some fellow will insist it must be hung in the sanctuary. And if a sermon is so poorly prepared that it is embarrassing to any man not deaf, blind, and illiterate, still there will be some who excuse it because the brother is kindly and well-meaning.

Shoddy stuff is still shoddy stuff even when it is taken to church.

You cannot baptize second-rate performances into excellence. Lousy poetry is still lousy poetry, though it have a religious theme. Everybody knows this except the soft-headed Christians who lose all critical sense when they hear an Amen. There must be more of such people than there ought to be, which may be the reason competent critics twinge with dread when they are told they are going to see a religious play or read a religious novel.

The Church at its best attracts the best. In the Middle Ages the great cathedrals received the best their generations could give. So we still journey far to see the windows, the towers, the pulpits made a thousand years ago to the glory of God. The Bible is not only great in its religion but it is a classic in literature. The *Book of Common Prayer* is not only a book of liturgy but a treasure house for those who love the English language.

It may be that in your congregation there are no artists and no musicians. Well then, leave the church plain and unadorned until you can have the best. If the choir cannot tell the difference between "Pop Goes the King" and "God Save the Weasel," then let the congregation sing a hymn. It will help if the sermon has great thoughts clothed in a lean and lucid style. For then the rest of the service will not be tolerated by the people unless it is marked with dignity and excellence.

As ministers of the Church, we have an obligation to raise the tastes of our people. A little pious covering will not be pleasing to either God or man. We ought to be men who can at least recognize and appreciate the best. Nothing is quite so bad as what is ill done in the name of our religion. The first sign of the presence of the Holy Spirit is a hunger in the heart for excellence.

# 55: *Accolades*

It is the season to be merry and appreciative, so if you will allow it, I would like to distribute a few well-deserved accolades. There is neither profit nor cash connected with these presents, and those to whom they are directed will probably be too busy even to notice. But it fills my heart with joy just to think of some of these saints, and it may help some of you to get through the commercialization and drunkenness which has become the American way of celebrating the Savior's birth.

First, I want to give kudos to the layman who seldom agrees with the social views of his minister, but never threatens to cut off his financial support or leave the church. This fellow is not properly appreciated, and he is the salt of the earth. He is that rare being who assumes that God sends prophets not to be targets for stones, but to be squirmed under and considered. He hears his cherished ideas challenged nearly every Sunday, and he never organizes a committee to oust the preacher. I'll tell you a secret. He has more grace and patience than I have, and I love him like a brother. May his tribe increase!

Secondly, a resolution of appreciation to the preacher who never allows personal opposition to split the congregation. He finds himself criticized for everything from driving the wrong car to wearing the wrong necktie. He is attacked for his theology by fundamentalists whose Christianity has turned to hate and bitterness. His concern for the poor and hungry is portrayed as subversion by the rightists and all the profit-making, professional anti-Communists. Yet he remains calm, and loves these smug Pharisees who are not worthy to tie his shoes. He remains pastor to all the people and moves among the psychotics like a physician in a mental sanitarium. He is a living witness to the truth that the spirit of the Bethlehem Child can possess a man.

In the third place, let me give a scroll of honor to the woman who has taught a Sunday-school class for the last twenty-five years. In spite of all the changing theories of religious education and the different materials she has had to use, she has never become discouraged. Whether we were emphasizing projects or permissiveness or play or even the Bible, she has continued. And through it all, she has managed by her own Christian character and deep faith to introduce generation after generation of children to Jesus Christ. These youngsters, some of them now with families of their own, rise up to call her blessed, and so do I.

Finally, let me present a plaque to the church custodian who has served the same congregation for ten years and still believes in God. He has set up chairs for a luncheon and then rearranged them because the chairman changed her mind. He has cleaned up after thoughtless youth groups who made a shambles of the social hall on Saturday night. He has been the confidant of the minister and never betrayed him. He has kept the air fresh in the sanctuary on Sunday morning and never opened or closed a window during the prayer, the anthem, or the sermon. In short, he has been a living demonstration of Christianity in action and an inspiration to both the laity and the ministry.

Dear brothers and sisters, God bless you every one!

*Set in Linotype Granjon*
*Composed, printed and bound by The Haddon Craftsmen, Inc.*
HARPER & ROW, PUBLISHERS, INCORPORATED